M. Skelly

BEHOLD YOUR KING

BEHOLD YOUR KING

Meditations in Matthew

J. M. FLANIGAN

JOHN RITCHIE LTD
CHRISTIAN PUBLICATIONS

40 Beansburn, Kilmarnock, Scotland

ISBN 1 904064 11 6

Copyright © 2002 by John Ritchie Ltd.,
40 Beansburn, Kilmarnock, Scotland

First Edition 2002

Printed by Bell & Bain Ltd., Glasgow

Contents

Foreword 7

Preface 9

Introduction 11

CHAPTER 1
   The King's Ancestry and Advent 15

CHAPTER 2
   Herod, the Wise Men, and the Innocents 22

CHAPTER 3
   The King's Ambassador 30

CHAPTER 4
   The Wilderness and the Early Ministry 34

CHAPTER 5
   The Sermon on the Mount 42

CHAPTER 6
   The Sermon on the Mount (continued) 49

CHAPTER 7
   The Sermon on the Mount (concluded) 53

CHAPTER 8
   Early Miracles 57

CHAPTER 9
   Further Miracles 61

CHAPTER 10
   The Charge to the Twelve 65

CHAPTER 11
   The Prophet in Prison 69

CHAPTER 12
   The King is Rejected 73

CHAPTER 13
The Kingdom Parables 77
CHAPTER 14
Martyrdom, Multitudes, and Miracles........................... 81
CHAPTER 15
Crumbs from the Table; Bread in the Wilderness......... 85
CHAPTER 16
The Great Confession... 89
CHAPTER 17
The Transfiguration.. 93
CHAPTER 18
Precepts and Parables 97
CHAPTER 19
The Return to Judea 101
CHAPTER 20
Service and Suffering 105
CHAPTER 21
The King, the Village, and the City................................ 111
CHAPTER 22
Pharisees, Sadducees, and Herodians 117
CHAPTER 23
Scribes, Pharisees, Hypocrites 123
CHAPTER 24
The Olivet Discourse 128
CHAPTER 25
The Olivet Discourse (continued) 134
CHAPTER 26
The Anointing, the Upper Room, the Betrayal, and
the Denial 139
CHAPTER 27
The Trial and Death of the King 145
CHAPTER 28
The Risen Master 151
CONCLUSION and SUMMARY 157

Foreword

Matthew could never have anticipated the outflow of blessing which would result, not only to himself but also to countless others, from his response to the call of Christ. His suitability to write the first Gospel has never been in doubt; after all he was a Jew, writing particularly to fellow Jews, about this apparent Stranger whose uniqueness had made such an impression on him. But while Matthew's record may not have been written *to* us, it was written *for* us, and many have been richly rewarded by careful study of his Gospel.

Jim Flanigan is a highly regarded teacher of the Scriptures in the assemblies among which he moves, and brings to his writings, not only a clear understanding of the text, but also his own inimitable way of expressing his thoughts.

Israel said, and continues to say, that "there is no beauty in Him that we should desire Him". Christians are those who have come to see Him as "the altogether lovely One". It is this unfading and incomparable beauty upon which our brother meditates in the twenty-eight chapters of this delightful work.

As the title indicates, the golden thread of our Lord's Kingship runs through the book. From the question asked by the wise men - "Where is he that is born King of the Jews?", to the superscription on the cross - "This is Jesus the King of the Jews", the reader will be both challenged and encouraged by the reminder that He who is Lord and Head of the Church is the One destined to reign over an everlasting kingdom.

E Taylor

Preface

These meditations in Matthew's Gospel first appeared as a series of articles in the "Assembly Testimony" magazine over a period of five years from 1995 to 1999.

At the request of many readers they are now published in book form. They have been slightly revised and their format has been altered a little, and they are sent forth with the prayer that they may be both profitable to the Lord's people and glorifying to the Lord Jesus.

The meditations have not been prepared particularly for students or scholars, though it is hoped that such may find help in them. But not all saints are students, and these papers have been written in such a way as to appeal to believers in the Lord Jesus everywhere, both young and old. They are indeed meditations rather than lessons or lectures.

We all, of course, delight to read and hear of the Saviour whom we love, and Matthew's Gospel is full of Him. Those of us who were but poor Gentiles have cause to be especially grateful. Israel's Messiah has become our Saviour and Lord, our Beloved and our Bridegroom, and all that has been written concerning Him is now precious to us. We are deeply indebted to Matthew, the converted publican and Jew, who knew Jesus so well, and who, by inspiration, has bequeathed to us such a delightful and magnificent treatise on the life and ministry of the Messiah. He has given us, too, a touching account of His sufferings, death, and resurrection.

It is sincerely hoped that our meditations will make the Saviour more precious to all who read them, and that, as we look forward in anticipation to His future reign, we may be able to pray intelligently, "Thy kingdom come". Meantime, Behold your King!

Jim Flanigan
Belfast
June, 2002

Introduction

As everyone knows, there are four Gospels. These present their several views of the Saviour in an inspired beauty of diversity and variety with harmony and unity. Many writers have attempted, over the years, to give us one uninterrupted "Life of Christ", arranging His miracles and parables and the course of His life and ministry in a consecutive order, just as it had been. This might be interesting, and in some senses helpful, yet we must remember that God could Himself have given us such an account in one single Gospel, had He been so minded. But such is the inscrutability of the Person of Christ that divine wisdom has deemed it necessary for us to have a fourfold, full-orbed presentation of Him, in order that we might, the more intelligently, in some little measure, catch suitable glimpses of His glory and appreciate Him. We must be grateful for the inspiration that has given us four Gospels, with no discrepancies, no mistakes, no contradictions, no inaccuracies, and no misrepresentations.

The four authors of the Gospels have been divinely chosen, and we shall have to notice in some detail the choice of Matthew for this first Gospel, the Gospel of the King and the Kingdom. To John Mark, whom we ever remember as the servant who lapsed for a little while (Acts 15.37-38), was given the privilege of writing the story of a Servant who never failed, the Perfect Servant. Luke, of our third Gospel, was a Physician, a Doctor who would have known men and human nature better than most. He gives us a portrait of the only perfect Man the world has ever seen, and his Gospel has accordingly been called "The loveliest book in the world". The fourth Gospel tells of a Son who ever dwells in the bosom of the Father. It was written by that beloved disciple who once lay on the bosom of the Son (Jn 13.25; 21.20).

It was kind and gracious of God to entrust the writing of this particular Gospel to Matthew. Matthew had been, after all, a publican, a tax collector for the hated Romans. Exacting taxes from one's own fellow-countrymen to fill the coffers of Caesar and his cohorts was a despicable thing. No self-respecting Jew would have done it. Rome had invaded Israel's land and subjugated her people. To work for Rome was a betrayal of Jewish hopes and aspirations. What Jew, with a true anticipation of a Messianic Kingdom, would have stooped to be in the employ of a foreign regime like Rome? But then, the publicans were men of little scruples, and there was monetary gain to be had in this tax collecting if one was unscrupulous. Publicans and sinners! The two were adjoined in one breath. And Matthew was a publican! Who would ever have thought that Matthew, tax collector for Caesar, would become the inspired biographer of the King of Israel? It was grace, grace alone, sovereign grace, that lifted him on that memorable day when Jesus called.

It seems reasonable to assume that Matthew had heard the Saviour preach before then, but on that day the general call of the gospel to the crowds who listened had become a particular call to Matthew. It was very personal. It was very direct. It was very brief. "Follow me" (Mt 9.9). Matthew's response was immediate, and the record of it is very brief too. "He arose, and followed him". Luke adds the telling comment, "He left all" (Lk 5.28). Someone has put the story of Matthew's conversion into poetry, as if Matthew would say-

> *I heard His call,*
> *Come, follow, that was all.*
> *My gold grew dim,*
> *My heart went after Him,*
> *I rose; I followed; that was all.*
> *Who would not follow*
> *If they heard His call?*

Matthew had met a Man whose life was lived on entirely opposite principles to his own. Daily he had sat on the roadway, somewhere outside Capernaum, demanding customs and taxes from the Galilean fishermen, perhaps even from Simon Peter himself! His message to them was, "Give! Give!". But in Jesus he had met Someone whose message to men was, "Come...I will give you" (Mt 11.28). It was so different. Grace wrought response in Matthew's heart. He left all for Jesus. Rome, Caesar, taxes, the old life, the gain, were all abandoned in a moment. Matthew had found a new Master and a new way.

The old publican would never forget that grace. It shines through his Gospel. There are instances of it through all the chapters. Matthew's other name was "Levi". Grace now lifted him to become a true son of Israel, and among all his apostolic privileges perhaps this was the greatest, that he should be chosen to write the story of Israel's King.

He introduces his Gospel as the book of the generation of Jesus the Messiah and immediately links the Name of Jesus with the names of David and Abraham. Here are allusions to the two great covenants. David and Abraham were the trustees of Jehovah's promises of a country and a kingdom, but here are the names of those two men who raised sons for the throne and the altar respectively. David's Solomon was destined to reign. Abraham's Isaac was destined to be offered up. Throne and altar indeed! Matthew's Gospel is but an exposition of this great principle, that the way to the crown is by the cross. The avenue to the throne leads by the altar. For Jesus the Messiah the pathway to glory would be by Golgotha. But the end was assured. Jesus is indeed the Christ, the Messiah. He is the Son of Abraham and must be offered up, but He is the Son of David and He must reign. He will inherit the kingdom, the throne, and the crown.

In the genealogy of the opening chapter, Matthew establishes the legal rights of Jesus to that throne and kingdom, and he does this in a manner which is detailed, interesting, and indisputable. We of this later day have lived to see so much of it all accomplished, and while the day of the vindication and coronation of the rejected King is still future, yet even now we can sing –

> *Man of sorrows, God of glory,*
> *Wondrous path Thy foot hath trod.*
> *Cross and crown rehearse the story,*
> *Joyous sound this note abroad –*
> *Calvary's victim*
> *Now adorns the throne of God.*

It is our privilege too, in this day of His rejection, to enthrone Him in our hearts and crown Him Lord of all, seeking to live for His honour, loyal and true to Him in the world that cast Him out.

CHAPTER 1

The King's Ancestry and Advent

It is perhaps well enough known that in the four Gospels there are two genealogies of the Lord Jesus. There is no genealogy in Mark. That is the Gospel of the Servant, and a genealogy would be neither appropriate nor relevant. There is no genealogy in John. That is the Gospel of the glory of the Son of God. It commences with a "beginningless beginning" where human genealogy is not possible. Matthew, however, paints a portrait of a King, and Luke presents the beauties of a perfect Man. The legal rights of that King must be established beyond all doubt, and it is needful also for Luke to trace the human lineage of that perfect Man. In these two Gospels genealogies are both necessary and welcome.

There is an acknowledged difficulty in the reconciling of the two genealogies and an explanation is needed. It will, of course, be easily and readily observed firstly, that the two genealogies move in opposite directions. Matthew's begins with Abraham and moves forward through David and Solomon eventually to Joseph, husband of Mary the virgin mother. Luke begins with Joseph and moves backward through David and Abraham to Adam. There is then, for a little, a common line in the two. From Abraham to David in Matthew agrees with David to Abraham in Luke. After David, however, there is a divergence, and for a very important reason.

Matthew's genealogy proceeds from David through His son Solomon. Luke will rather trace the line through David's other son Nathan (see 2 Sam 5.14). The reason for this digression becomes apparent from Jeremiah 22.30. Jechonias, of Solomon's seed, is cursed and disinherited. He is reckoned as if childless, without heir, and Joseph is of that line. So our Lord's lineage may be traced in another way. Joseph is "son" (in-law?) of Mary's father Heli. Jesus is therefore Joseph's heir, but He is not of Solomon's line but of Nathan's. He is Son of David but He is not Son of Solomon. Had He been so descended from Solomon He would have inherited the curse on Jechonias. The Lord Jesus, born of a virgin, inherits the title to the throne, but not the curse on Solomon's seed.

Now note the orderliness of Matthew's genealogy. He will reckon the generations in three series. From Abraham to David is the first series. Then from David to the carrying away into Babylon. Then from the captivity to Christ. It has been said that he is following the line from Israel's morning to Israel's noon, and on to Israel's evening. In each period he will list fourteen generations, but note the inspired accuracy of Holy Scripture. Matthew says that "all" the generations from Abraham to David are fourteen. Notice the careful inclusion of the little word "all" in the first series, but its omission from the second and third series. He does not say that "all" the generations from David to the carrying away into Babylon are fourteen. He simply states that we may observe fourteen generations in that period. The reason for the omission of the word "all" here is, of course, that not all the generations of that period are listed. There was a wicked Queen, Athaliah, daughter of Ahab, who once had tried to destroy the seed royal (2 Chr 22.10). The names of her immediate progeny are omitted, as Ahaziah, Joash, and Amaziah, leaving fourteen generations as Matthew gives them. This is divine accuracy. Matthew knew that any intelligent Hebrew could verify the authenticity of the genealogy. He was not manipulating the history of the nation or attempting to mislead. Nor was he constructing an inaccurate lineage of Jesus. Other genealogical lists were then available in the Jewish archives to confirm the truth of what he was saying.

Now it has often been pointed out that Matthew's inclusion of five women in the genealogy is very touching. And such women as four of them were! Tamar! Rahab! Ruth! Bathsheba! Tamar and Bathsheba were adulteresses. Rahab was a Canaanitess. Ruth was a Moabitess. Is Matthew emphasising that same grace that had reached him as a publican? Tamar's is an unsavoury story of deceit and immorality and shame. Rahab is ever remembered as "Rahab the harlot". Ruth had been an idolater from Moab. Bathsheba had been complicit in David's awful sin of adultery which had led on to murder. We are reminded that she had been the wife of Urias. Yet, in sovereign grace, these four women are here included in the lineage of the Messiah.

Someone has beautifully remarked that grace reaches sinners like Tamar, on the ground of redemption as seen in Ruth, on the principle of faith as seen in Rahab, to raise to a position of glory as seen in Bathsheba.

The fifth woman is, of course, that pious maiden from Nazareth, who bowed her will to the will of God, and, accepting the inevitable reproach and scorn, became the virgin mother of the Messiah. Of Mary it would be said, "Blessed art thou among women".

The grace that had reached these women was indeed the same sovereign grace that had reached Matthew the publican. This is the grace that has reached us too. Most of us were in Gentile darkness and insignificance. We had no claims upon God, and no rights at all. We were strangers like Ruth and Rahab. We were sinners like Tamar and Bathsheba. The grace that brought these women into the genealogy of the King, and that made Matthew the tax collector the King's biographer, has brought us to be His royal bride, and His companion in the glory of the coming kingdom. "O the depth of the riches both of the wisdom and knowledge of God! How unsearchable are his judgments, and his ways past finding out!" (Rom 11.33). Well do we sing –

> *Oh, this uttermost salvation,*
> *'Tis a fountain full and free,*
> *Pure, exhaustless, ever flowing,*
> *Wondrous grace, it reaches me.*
> *It reaches me. It reaches me.*
> *Wondrous grace, it reaches me.*

Having proven the title of Jesus to the throne of David, Matthew will now write of the miracle of our Lord's virgin conception and birth. "Jesus" is the New Testament Greek form of the Old Testament Hebrew "Joshua". There had been two Joshuas in Israel's history. One was that captain of Israel's armies who had led them into the Promised Land. He had done what Moses the lawgiver had not been permitted to do. The other Joshua was High Priest when the remnant nation came back from Babylon to settle in the land again (Zech 3). Jesus is our Joshua. He is the Captain of our salvation and also our great High Priest (Heb 2.10,17).

It has been well said that the mystery of the Saviour's incarnation is to be adored, not pried into. If we cannot understand how, in the natural process, the bones are formed in the womb (Eccl 11.5); if we cannot tell how we who are naturally conceived are made in secret and curiously wrought (Ps 139.13-16); how can we be expected to understand the mystery of our Lord's miraculous conception by the Holy Spirit in the womb of the virgin? We may not indeed understand, but, nevertheless, the virgin birth of the Lord Jesus is clearly taught in the Scriptures, and where we cannot understand we can still wonder and worship.

There are at least three attitudes among men to the truth of the virgin birth. Some there are who personally believe it and accept it, but who do not require that others should believe it.

They argue that it is optional and not fundamental. Others there are who deny the truth of it absolutely. They blasphemously rank it with folklore and fable, and reject it totally. Many of us, however, believe it, and believe it to be foundational and, indeed, fundamental. To deny this truth is to deny the integrity of godly persons, as Mary, Joseph, Luke, and Matthew. To deny it is to deny the inspiration of the written Word of God, which not only predicted it, but recorded the accurate fulfilment of those predictions. To deny it is to deny also the essential holiness of the Living Word Himself, who, of necessity, must come into our world voluntarily and uniquely, the Seed of the woman, taking part of flesh and blood of His own volition. By a miraculous conception, wrought by the ministration of the Holy Spirit, He came amongst us, having no link with fallen Adam such as we have. How clear is that word to Mary: "The Holy Spirit shall come upon thee, and the power of the Highest shall overshadow thee: therefore also that holy thing that shall be born of thee shall be called the Son of God" (Lk 1.35). Let infidel scholars argue as they may over the Hebrew word ALMA, which is translated "virgin" in Matthew 1.23. Although there can be no reasonable doubt about the translation, the truth of our Lord's virgin birth is not dependent upon one word. It is the clear and unambiguous testimony of those early narratives, and the true believer accepts it implicitly.

Mary was, at this time, the betrothed wife of Joseph. They were contracted. They were solemnly pledged the one to the other, and it was during this period of betrothal that Mary was found to be with child. It is important to note that Joseph is already called her "husband" and Mary is already called his "wife" (Mt 1.20,24), and this though they had not yet come together physically. Their husband-wife relationship was a contract, to be culminated in a physical union but not dependent upon that union, and it could at that stage be severed only by a solemn and legal "putting away" - a divorce. Unchastity during this betrothal period was the only ground which our Lord recognised for such putting away (Mt 5.32).

If, as is suggested by some, it is the physical act which constitutes the marriage, then we would be faced with the unthinkable situation that Jesus was born out of wedlock, for it was not until after His birth that this "husband and wife", Joseph and Mary, came together as such.

It must have been a profound shock and disappointment to Joseph to learn of Mary's condition. He was a righteous man, and no doubt he had espoused the lowly maiden from Nazareth because of her piety. But he was, too, like those other Josephs, a good man (Lk 23.50; Acts 11.24), and being such a man he would deal gently and compassionately with the maid. His righteousness required that he must put her away, but even the law at times dealt charitably with such cases as Joseph now supposes (Deut 22.26), and Joseph resolves to put Mary away as quietly as possible.

Then, while he pondered in his perplexity, an angelic visitation brought relief to him. Not "the" angel of the Lord, as in our AV, but "an" angel of the Lord. "The" angel of the Lord was even now in the womb of the virgin! In a dream the word comes to Joseph, "Fear not...". This is the first of five dreams in these first two chapters of Matthew's Gospel. (See also 2.12,13,19,22).

The angel addresses Joseph in dignified terms, calling him "son of David". He may be but a carpenter of Nazareth, but he is a son of David with a place in God's purpose and plan. Perhaps there is a reminder here to us, that even in our humble status, and lowly station in life, there is a divine pattern for our lives and a privileged role for us in heaven's plan.

Mary's Child has been begotten by the Holy Spirit. The Seed of the woman will soon make His advent, and Mary is His chosen vessel. The Child will be the fruit of her womb (Lk 1.42). Luke the Doctor will give a more detailed account of those early days, and of Mary's visit to her cousin Elizabeth, but

Matthew, in accord with the theme and character of his Gospel, will tell us that it all came to pass that the Scriptures might be fulfilled. Here is a specific reference to Isaiah 7.14, and it will be a feature of Matthew that he will keep quoting Old Testament Scriptures.

Someone has said that Matthew's Gospel is like a mighty tree, with uncountable twigs and branches reaching upward into the new dispensation and the millennium, but with massive roots sunk deeply into Old Testament prophecies. This indeed is how it is.

Joseph awakes from his dream. The Child will be Emmanuel – "God with us". Mary's firstborn Son will be Incarnate Deity. Jesus, Saviour of His people from their sins, is none other than Jehovah of the Old Testament and of Israel's history. Joseph does as he is bidden, and so the delightful story unfolds. The desire expressed in that simple hymn of our childhood is indeed so very relevant –

> *Tell me the story of Jesus,*
> *Write on my heart every word,*
> *Tell me the story most precious,*
> *Sweetest that ever was heard.*

CHAPTER 2

Herod, the Wise Men, and the Innocents

When Jesus was born in Bethlehem there was a usurper on the throne. Herod was an Edomite, with no legal entitlement to the crown which he wore. He was a puppet king who had been enthroned by Rome. "Herod the Great" they called him. He was indeed a great builder, and relics of his work remain until this day. But, as he later demonstrated in what has been termed "the slaughter of the innocents", he was great chiefly for his evil; a cruel man, as most of the Herods were.

At the time of the Saviour's birth certain magi, wise men, arrived from the East. How many there were we do not know. Having seen the star which told them of Messiah's birth, they had travelled from their homeland, whether Arabia, Persia, or Babylon, we cannot tell. Balaam had prophesied of a star, and he had been from the East, from Pethor by the Euphrates in Mesopotamia (Num 22.5; 24.17). Did they know of Balaam and his prophecy?

It is important to note that there are two Bethlehems in Israel. Observe how Matthew, with the prophets, identifies the correct Bethlehem. It is "Bethlehem of Judea"; "Bethlehem Ephratah"; "Bethlehem in the land of Juda". There is a Bethlehem in Galilee, not many miles from Nazareth, but Matthew and Luke and the prophets direct us again and again to that Bethlehem of Judea, some five or six miles south of Jerusalem. It is this Bethlehem that Micah predicts as the birthplace of the Messiah (Mic 5.2).

The wise men, however, did not come to Bethlehem, but to Jerusalem. Jerusalem was, after all, the Capital City, and one might expect to find the King there. These magi did not, as is often suggested, follow the star all across the miles from their Eastern homeland to Jerusalem. The star had appeared, not initially to guide them, but to indicate that the King had been born. It was then, having seen the star, that they began the long journey to Jerusalem.

Having arrived at the Capital they ask what is now the first question in our New Testament, "Where is he?". What a delightful question. Is not the rest of the New Testament but an expanded answer to this? Surely this is the spirit in which we must approach our reading and study of the Scriptures: "Where is He?". We shall never be disappointed if we come to our reading with such a mind, looking for Him. Wise men always look for Him and the Scriptures always give clear directions to the sincere enquirer. Herod, though, is troubled at the news that certain magi from the East have come to look for a new-born King of the Jews. Herod, Edomite that he was, never did feel secure on the throne. There is a sad irony here, that Gentiles from the East have come to see and to worship the Messiah, and yet Herod and all Jerusalem are troubled about it.

Herod calls together the chief priests and scribes. These were the men, after all, who knew all about worship, and about the Scriptures, and about the Messiah. Or at least they should have known. They did indeed know of Micah's prophecy, and they assured Herod that Bethlehem of Judea was the predicted birthplace of the Christ. Out of this Bethlehem, with its relative insignificance, was to come the great Shepherd-Governor of Israel. The birth of Messiah was to give dignity to the place of His birth. Bethlehem, with its memories of Rachel, of Ruth, and of David, was to be the Bethlehem of the Christ.

Having so consulted the priests and scribes, Herod now

summons the wise men. He calls them privily, quietly, secretly, to ask for an accurate timing of the appearance of the star. He sends them to Bethlehem and, in deceit, he expresses his lying concern that when they have found the Child they should bring him word so that he too could come and pay homage. It was gross hypocrisy, for he had evil ulterior motives. However, it is now that the star reappears and the wise men rejoice to see it again. Now it goes before them, and they follow, until it stands over the house where the young Child is. Notice that it is not now "the babe" (as in Luke 2), but "the young child". It is a different word, indicating the holy development of the Infant Messiah. Notice, too, that Matthew always speaks of "the young child and his mother". Some five times he repeats this. It is never "the mother and the child". Others may say that, but never Matthew. For Matthew, and for those who truly love the Saviour, the Holy Child must have precedence. It is always "the young child and his mother".

What an example is this star for those who would be servants of Christ. Its sole ministry is to direct men to the Saviour, and when once that ministry has been accomplished and men have found Him, then the star will disappear, never to be seen again. The true evangelist will give the light that shows the way to Christ, and then, like the star, be content not to be seen again.

If the star gives us an example of godly witness, then the wise men give us an example of true worship. Here is the first reference to worship in the New Testament. The wise men open their treasures. Matthew speaks of treasure more than any of the other Gospel writers. He speaks of treasures which are material and temporal, of those which are moral and spiritual and eternal, and of those which are dispensational and ministerial. It is a rewarding exercise for the believer to search for these treasures in Matthew's Gospel. There are nine such references. Little did these worshippers from the East know just how far-reaching the effects of their worship would be. They could hardly have known the rich symbolic significance of the treasures that they brought. They presented their gifts. Observe that they worshipped "Him". Mary was there, of course, in quiet and dutiful attendance, but the wise men worshipped the Child. "Blessed art thou among women", Gabriel had said to Mary (Lk 1.28), but the wise men paid homage to the Infant Saviour, not to Mary. Was this to be an early rebuke to the Mariolatry of a later day, an error which would have grieved Mary herself?

From their treasures the worshippers presented gold, frankincense, and myrrh. Do we not present the same as we bring our appreciation of Christ to God in worship? We bring the gold of His personal glory. Gold was the most precious mineral that men then knew. How much of it appears in the symbolism of the tabernacle and the temple. It seems ever to speak of the glory of deity to us, when used symbolically of Christ. We rejoice in this, the glory of a Son in equality with the Father. It is our privilege to bring to God, in our priestly exercises, our appreciation of the eternal glory of the Son.

Then there was the frankincense. It was pure, white, and fragrant. It is a most fitting symbol of the moral glory of the Saviour. In Him there was a unique preciousness, in that He alone among men, was sinlessly pure, incomparable and impeccable, holy and harmless. Here, in those early infant days, there was already a sweet foreshadowing of that lovely life that was to follow.

But there was a mingling of bitterness with the sweetness. They presented myrrh. This was sweet to the smell but bitter to the taste. How sweet to those who love Him is the remembrance of the sufferings of the Man of Sorrows, but how bitter those sufferings were to Him. We love and adore as we ponder on the sorrows of that last long night of suffering. What memories! The physical pain and the mockery, the thorny crown, the scourge, the buffeting, the nails, the thirst, the darkness and the spear. These draw out the heart of every believer in the fragrance of worship.

We too, then, bring our gold and frankincense and myrrh. Those wise men were not to know that more than twenty centuries later, countless adoring hearts would come, as they did, to open their treasures and present their gifts, and then walk a path diverse from the world around which knows Him not. The magi were warned of God to take another way. J N Darby says that the expression "warned of God" has the thought of divine instruction, and that it signifies an answer after consultation. Did the wise men have their doubts about the sincerity of Herod? There was a divine and timely answer. It was not merely a warning, but an oracle of instruction from God to them. They obeyed, forsook Herod, and left for their own country by another way.

After the departure of the wise men Joseph is warned in a dream of the evil intention of Herod to destroy the Child, and there follows what has been called, "The flight into Egypt". In obedience to the heavenly directive Joseph rises in the night hours and takes the young Child and His mother to the south and to safety. The little family will sojourn in Egypt until the death of Herod and it may well be that the gifts of the wise men were Jehovah's provision for the sustenance of the family during this period of their exile.

Matthew, in keeping with the tenor of his Gospel, reminds us that this time spent in Egypt was yet another fulfilment of prophecy. It is an instance of the versatility and infinity of the inspired Word, for the prophecy of which Matthew speaks was in fact an historical reference to Israel. As it had been with the nation, so would it be with Jesus, "Out of Egypt have I called my son" (Hos 11.1). Matthew, by inspiration, takes that which was written of the nation and interprets it with reference to Christ. Meantime, Herod realises that the magi are not returning to him, and he is enraged. Somewhere, the Infant, the true King of Israel, is lying serene and at peace, while Herod and all Jerusalem with him are disturbed and troubled. He issues the awful edict, so reminiscent of the decree of Pharaoh centuries earlier in Exodus 1.15-22. All the infant boys, from two years old and under, in Bethlehem and in all its borders, were to be slain. According to the time which he had accurately assessed from the wise men, Herod estimated that the Infant King could not be more than two years old. The star had appeared when the Child was born. He had to take into account the travelling time from the East to Jerusalem, and he reasoned that if all the male children under two years in the environs of Bethlehem were slain, then the Infant in question would be slain with them. It was a heartless cruel edict indeed. Herod the Great they called him! Was this greatness, to take the innocents from the breasts of their weeping mothers and slay them, just to allay his own fears? Is Herod the Great to be remembered for this? Afraid? Of a little One?

There follows the awful massacre of the little boys, and yet again Matthew appeals to Holy Scripture. A voice is heard in Bethlehem, as it had been in Ramah in Jeremiah 31.15. There is weeping and great lamentation. Rachel weeping for her children. Rachel, that revered mother of old, that fitting symbol of Jewish motherhood, weeping inconsolably for her little ones.

The land is in deep mourning. Children's voices are silent, childish laughter is no more, and the mothers of Bethlehem, cruelly bereft of their children, refuse to be comforted. But in the purpose of God, as it had been with Moses in the days of Pharaoh, the Infant Christ whose death Herod had planned, is safely on His way out of Judea, south from Bethlehem, towards Egypt and sanctuary.

It is beautiful to read, twice in these verses, of "the land of Israel". The land which had become but a despised province of Rome, which was now ruled by Gentiles, which was in large part inhabited by Samaritans, the land whose Galilee had become known as Galilee of the nations, was, nevertheless, the land of Israel. It was Immanuel's land, and would be spoken of with this title of its dignity.

There is now a problem. They came and dwelt in Nazareth

"that it might be fulfilled which was spoken by the prophets, He shall be called a Nazarene". Our Lord was to live the greater part of His life here, the most of thirty years. But where in prophecy is it recorded of the Messiah that "He shall be called a Nazarene"? Since Nazareth is never once mentioned in the Old Testament, this presents a difficulty and several explanations have been offered.

Some will emphasise the word "spoken", and suggest that Matthew is not referring to any "written" prophecy at all, but is citing some verbal prediction which had been handed down orally from prophet to prophet through the generations. Others, perhaps a majority, will point out that the Hebrew word for "Branch" is NETSER (see e.g. Isaiah 11.1). This is, of course, a title of the Messiah. It is thought by many expositors that there is a correspondence between NETSER and "Nazareth", and that those Scriptures which refer to our Lord as "the Branch" are indicating that He would indeed be known as "the Nazarene". There is however, yet another explanation. Notice that the word "prophets" is in the plural. Matthew is not therefore quoting any one particular prophet or prophecy. Now, what the prophets all predicted was that Messiah would be, in the words of Isaiah, "despised and rejected". This was the common theme of so many of the Messianic prophecies, and so that this would be fulfilled our Lord chose to live in Nazareth and be called a Nazarene. Matthew 2.23 may refer to a prophetic theme rather than to a specific prediction.

Nazareth! A town of ill repute in lower Galilee. It is never mentioned in the Old Testament, nor even in the Apocrypha, or in the Talmud, or in Josephus. Both theologically and geographically it was outside the mainstream of Jewish life. Well do we speak of our Lord's early life as the years of obscurity. Nazareth was, however, a frontier town on the borders of Zebulun and close to several of the main trade routes. It was a stopping place for the night for merchants and traders from the North and from Gilead. This sadly contributed to the corruption of the town. They made it a nest of immorality and vice. The Saviour was to live here, in a defiled and defiling society, but Himself pure and untouched by the moral corruption which was all around. Nazareth, where He was brought up (Lk 4.16). "Can there any good thing come out of Nazareth?", asked one who knew it well. Nathanael lived at Cana, only but a few miles from Nazareth. In reply to his honest question, Philip says, "Come and see" (Jn 1.46). What blessedness indeed has come to us from Nazareth.

Twenty times afterwards in our New Testament the Saviour is called "Jesus of Nazareth" or "Jesus the Nazarene". His early disciples became known as "The sect of the Nazarenes" (Acts 24.5). It was a term of reproach, but He bore it with honour, and when Saul of Tarsus, blinded by the glory on the Damascus Road, asked, "Who art thou, Lord?" the answer was, "I am Jesus of Nazareth" (Acts 22.8).He carried the title with Him even into glory and His people delight to sing-

> *I stand amazed in the presence*
> *Of Jesus the Nazarene,*
> *And wonder how He could love me,*
> *A sinner condemned, unclean.*

CHAPTER 3

The King's Ambassador

Thirty years have now passed since the events of Chapters 1 and 2. The King has lived unknown and unrecognised in Galilee, but the time has now come for His manifestation to Israel, and, accordingly, His herald will prepare the way.

John Baptist has been likened to Elijah. Indeed it was in the spirit of that prophet that he had come (Mt 11.13-14). In his dress, in his diet, in his dwelling, and in his deportment, he was so like Elijah. His preaching was a wilderness ministry. He ministered in a dry ground where there was little fruit for God. John did not preach in the city. If Jerusalem would hear him then Jerusalem must go to him in the wilderness. This was the character of the man and his ministry. He was a voice crying in the wilderness.

John's preaching was plain and powerful. There was an urgency with it too. The Kingdom of the Heavens was at hand, and in view of this John had but one purpose in life. He demanded a preparation for the coming of the King. John's cloak of camel hair and his girdle of leather were in keeping with his message. There was no finery or worldly appeal, and there would be no yielding either. His food was plain too. He ate locusts and wild honey. There may have been, as some think, a locust tree, bearing edible pods. It is possible that these may have been his food rather than the locust that we naturally and normally think of. But, in any case, the locust as we know it was clean to eat, and it is specifically mentioned in Israel's dietary laws in Leviticus 11.22. There were, too, wild bees of the woods and the wilderness, providing honey as in Exodus 3.8 and 1 Samuel 14.26. John did not eat with men or socialise with them (Mt 11.18). He was a man apart, separated and dedicated to his unique ministry as the forerunner of the Messiah.

Many went out to John from the city and from the province. Those who responded to his message were baptised by him in the River Jordan. Jordan was, in symbol, the river of death and judgment, and John's baptism was an act of repentance, a confession of sins, an acknowledgment that sins deserved death. But then, as well as the common people, there came also Pharisees and Sadducees to the baptism. No doubt they came to see the strange prophet and to analyse and criticise his ministry. John was severe with them. They were a generation of vipers. They were as cunning and as poisonous as that old Serpent himself. Why had they come? Who had warned them to flee from the wrath to come? John demanded repentance, and evidence of it. To boast that Abraham was their forefather would not avail. God could raise up children to Abraham from the very stones that lay round about them. God would indeed move in judgment against them. He would cut down the fruitless among them. Like as an axe felled the trees they would be hewn down, and destroyed in the ensuing fire.

John's ministry was, in the main, a ministry of law. It exposed and denounced sin. It revealed a man's great need, and warned of coming judgment. But John's greatest ministry was to introduce Christ. The coming One was greater than the forerunner. He would be as one winnowing on the threshing floor, gathering in the wheat and driving away the chaff. John baptised with water, but the Messiah would baptise with the Holy Spirit and with fire. John here brings together two events which are separated in time by many centuries. The Day of Pentecost and the Day of Judgment, of which John here speaks, may be far apart in actual fulfilment, but in the preaching and in the purpose of God they were both assured.

"Then", as John was so preaching, Jesus came. The Coming One had arrived from Galilee. With no sins to confess and with no need of repentance, He would, nevertheless, take His place with a remnant people and stand with them in the waters of death. Was this a foreshadowing of that later day when, at Golgotha, He would be numbered with the transgressors, Himself a sinless Man? John protests at the Saviour's request for baptism. It ought to be the other way, he says, that the King should baptise the herald, that Messiah should baptise the forerunner. But Jesus insists. It was becoming that, together, the King and His herald should fulfil all righteousness, and so, together, the Baptist and his Lord stood in the Jordan. It has been said that the Good Shepherd saw His sheep going into the dark waters and he would fain go with them.

John's ministry, though brief, was now drawing to a close. The porter was opening the door for the Shepherd. John was a burning and a shining lamp, but the lamp must be extinguished when the Light appears. The law and the prophets were until John, but now the long promised Messiah and Saviour had come and the law and the prophets must withdraw. John's ministry is at an end.

The heavens were opened. As Jesus went up out of the water the Spirit of God descended like a dove and abode upon Him. It is another John who observes that it was at that time that the Saviour was pointed out as the Lamb of God (Jn 1.29). The gentle, heavenly Dove descends to rest upon the meek and lowly Lamb. Then, lo, a voice from the opened heaven. There are two voices in this chapter (vv.3,17). One voice is human, and the other is divine. One is from the wilderness, and the other is from the heavens. One is the voice of the forerunner, and the other is the voice of the Father. But the voices agree. They both speak well of Christ and draw attention to Him. Good is it for that preacher whose voice is in harmony with the voice of God, and whose message accords with the message of heaven.

"This is my beloved Son", the Father proclaims. Jesus of Nazareth, Jesus the Son of Mary, is the Son of the Father, the Son of God, the Beloved. So it was, that in those earliest moments of His years of public ministry, there was a heavenly approval of the Lord Jesus. "In whom I am well pleased". "In whom is all my delight".

Thirty years of pleasure He had given to His Father in Nazareth. The Father's tribute here is retrospective. It is an appreciation of those thirty delightful years, when, in the parched and barren ground that was Israel, there grew up before Him a tender plant, fragrant and beautiful, bringing immeasurable pleasure to God's heart.

> *All His joy, His rest, His pleasure,*
> *All His deep delight in Thee;*
> *Lord, Thy heart alone can measure*
> *What Thy Father found in Thee.*

It is the believer's high privilege to share the Father's delight in His Son. It is our joy to commune with God concerning the beauties and excellencies of Christ. "Truly our fellowship is with the Father" (1 Jn 1.3). May we ever increase and abound in our knowledge of the Saviour and in our desires after Him who is the Beloved, the joy of His Father's heart, and our Beloved too. The Adversary, however, is near at hand, as we shall see in the ensuing chapter.

CHAPTER 4

The Wilderness and the Early Ministry

This chapter begins with "Then", and we must ask, "When?". The answer is most important to a full appreciation of the scene that follows. It was just when heaven had been opened in approval of the Saviour. It was when the Spirit had descended in holy complacency upon Him. It was when the Father had proclaimed His delight in His Son. It was then, just then, that Jesus was led into the wilderness to the confrontation with the Devil, the archenemy. The heavenly approval provokes Satanic attack. Like as the first man had been tested in the garden, and had failed, so would the second Man be tested in the wilderness, but could not fail (Is 42.4).

After forty days and forty nights, almost six weeks of fasting, Jesus is hungry, and it is just now that the tempter comes to Him. It is essential to understand that the word "tempted" is used in two different ways in Scripture. It must be, for in one place James avows that God cannot be tempted with evil, and neither does He tempt any man (Jas 1.13), yet in another place we read that God did tempt Abraham (Gen 22.1), and in yet another place we have God's complaint to the Hebrews that their fathers had tempted Him in the desert (Heb 3.9).

Sometimes the word "tempted" may indeed imply a seduction, an enticement, an inducement to sin. Such temptation may often be true of us, but it can never, never, be true of the impeccable Christ. At other times, however, the word signifies a testing, a proving, as when gold might be tried in the fire to confirm its purity. Our Lord Jesus could never be enticed to sin, but in His wilderness experience He was tried in a three-fold way. He was tested as to His dependence, His obedience, and His patience. The testing but demonstrates His absolute freedom from sin and from the possibility of it. Had He not just been pointed out as the Lamb of God? He is therefore, He must be, a Lamb without blemish and without spot, in every way pure.

The tempter begins, characteristically, with an expression of doubt: "If…". "If thou be the Son of God…". This was, as in the Garden of Eden, a blatant slight on God's word. That word had just declared, "This is my beloved Son". The Devil says, "If thou be the Son...". It is the prelude to a triple temptation, leading on and up to an arrogant offer of world dominion in exchange for an expression of worship.

Our Lord then is to be tested as to His dependence. Is He hungry? "Command that these stones be made bread", says the tempter. And why should He not do so? He had the right, and the power, and He would, in a little while, turn water into wine for others. Why should He not now, a hungry Man, turn stones into bread for Himself? But then, had He not voluntarily assumed dependent manhood? It would not be in keeping with this dependency that He should act independently to meet His own need of the hour. He would continue to trust Him whom He had ever trusted (Ps 22.8-10). So He used the sword of the Spirit to repel the tempter, quoting from the Book of Deuteronomy. "Man shall not live by bread alone, but by every word that proceedeth out of the mouth of God (Deut 8.3).

The Saviour is then tested as to His obedience. Does He indeed quote Scripture? Then Satan will quote Scripture too, or misquote, as he did in Eden. On the pinnacle of the temple, on that highest point of the temple mount in the holy City, the Devil urges, "Cast thyself down", and then refers to the lovely

Psalm 91. But His quotation of the Word is incomplete, and the application irrelevant. "It is written", Jesus had said. "It is written", Satan now enjoins, quoting from the Psalm, but he omits the words "in all thy ways".Our Lord replies with yet another quotation. "It is written again", He says, and again He quotes from Deuteronomy (6.16). To cast oneself down needlessly into the depths of the Kidron Valley from that pinnacle point would not be trust. It would be but a spectacular tempting of the providence of God, not at all envisaged in the promise of Psalm 91.11-12. The obedient One would not be guilty of this and Satan is rebuffed again.

A third time the tempter comes, now to try our Lord's patience. From the vantage point of an exceeding high mountain the Saviour is shown all the kingdoms of the world and their glory. The treasures of Egypt, the might of Babylon, the culture of Greece, and the power of Rome, were all, in some way, displayed before His gaze in a dazzling panorama. "All these things will I give thee", Satan promised, "if thou wilt fall down and worship me". Surely the tempter must have known that our Lord was already the appointed heir of all things. Had he so soon forgotten that all things had been created by Him and for Him? And had not Jehovah in an ancient Psalm declared to the Son, "Ask of me, and I shall give thee the heathen for thine inheritance, and the uttermost parts of the earth for thy possession"? (Ps 2.8). With yet another quotation from Deuteronomy (6.13), Jesus repels the tempter again, saying, "Get thee hence, Satan". Our Lord refused from the Devil what the Man of Sin will accept, for when he comes he will be enthroned and empowered by Satan himself (Rev 13.2).

The rightful heir can wait in patience. He is at the Father's right hand now, sharing His Father's throne. He will wait expectantly until His enemies are made His footstool. Then he must reign, and the cry of many voices will echo throughout the heavens, "The kingdoms of this world are become the kingdoms of our Lord, and of his Christ (Rev 11.15). That which

He had refused from the hand of the tempter He will receive from the hand of His Father at the appointed time.

This record of the temptation in the wilderness is the solemn story of a connecting period between our Lord's private and public life. Thirty years in the relative obscurity of Nazareth and three years of busy public ministry are joined together by forty days of trial in the loneliness of the Judean desert. There is perhaps a lesson here for every servant of God. The years of our service are properly preceded by valuable years of preparation, when we may of necessity be occupied with things familial and secular. There is, however, a time of lonely exercise and patient waiting upon God, during which time the servant inevitably becomes the object of Satanic interest and onslaught. Such experiences, irksome though they may be, are undoubtedly used of God to equip His servants for their future ministry. Moses had his years in the backside of the desert. Paul had his time of waiting in Arabia. So the Saviour Himself, God's perfect Servant, after thirty years in Nazareth, spent forty days in the wilderness. He has left us an example that we should follow His steps.

In the early days of His ministry the Lord Jesus left Nazareth to make His home in Capernaum. On that memorable day when He had read Isaiah 61 in the Nazareth synagogue, they had rejected Him. He had read the passage to them and had presented Himself to them as the Messiah of whom the prophet had written, but they had refused Him. They indeed rejected Him forcibly and would have cast Him over the brow of the hill on which Nazareth was built, but He had passed quietly through the crowd and made His way to Capernaum to reside there. In character with his Gospel, Matthew sees here another fulfilment of prophecy. Capernaum was by the sea, in the region of the territories of Zebulun and Naphtali, and Isaiah had specifically mentioned these in relation to Messiah's ministry, saying of them that "The people that walked in darkness have seen a great light: they that dwell in the land of the shadow of death, upon them hath the light shined" (Is 9.1-2). Capernaum began to be privileged above many other cities, in that Messiah actually lived there. It became known as "his own city" (Mt 9.1). He walked its streets and wrought mighty works in it. Capernaum was indeed exalted to heaven, but its rejection of the Saviour was to bring it from the heights of privilege down to disaster and ruin. Today it is but a heap of black stone. The ruins of its synagogue stand to this day as a gaunt monument to its unbelief.

> *Tell me, ye mouldering fragments, tell,*
> *Was the Saviour's city here?*
> *Lifted to heaven, has it sunk to hell,*
> *With none to shed a tear?*

From Capernaum Jesus began to travel through all Galilee, preaching the glad tidings, calling for repentance, and announcing the Kingdom of Heaven. The King had come!

Walking along the shores of the Sea of Galilee on one of those days, He called His earliest disciples, the brothers Peter and Andrew. They were fishermen. When He called them they were casting their nets into the sea. It was doubtless a symbolic foreshadowing of the spiritual ministry that He had in mind for them, for they were to become fishers of men. Andrew, however, would perhaps fish more often with a line, as it were. He would minister personally to individuals, so that ever afterwards when we read of him, he is bringing men to Christ. His brother Peter would fish with a net, appealing to the multitudes, preaching to the crowds, drawing in as many as three thousand souls on the day of Pentecost in Acts 2.

"Follow me", the Saviour had called, and in an immediate response they left their nets and followed Him. The call of another two brothers seems to follow soon after. James and John were mending their nets. Was this too a foreshadowing of a future ministry? We need men like Peter and Andrew, to be fishers in gospel activity, and we are grateful for so many brethren who do just that. But we also need men like James and John, men who will bring a ministry of mending, a ministry that will heal differences and repair schisms, and generally help to maintain the testimony in a healthy and happy condition.

In a scene of unbelief how refreshing it must have been to the Saviour that there were those who would respond to His call and so readily follow Him. Like so many devoted servants of His ever since, these men left business and family to follow the Master. There were, of course, to be failings, lapses, shortcomings, but how much, nevertheless, He appreciated their company, their fellowship, their trust. It is still so. He still calls. In a world that has rejected Him He still looks for those who will obey His call and follow Him in loving service.

Matthew uses an expression which so beautifully and aptly sums up our Lord's ministry. "Jesus went about all Galilee, teaching...preaching...healing". It was a gracious ministry. It has been said that in teaching He expounded the message; in preaching He applied the message; in healing He illustrated the message. But soon His fame was to go far beyond Galilee. It went over Israel's northern border into Syria, and there were brought to Him for healing the diseased and the demon possessed, those that were physically ill and those that were mentally and spiritually ill. What memorable days those were! The whole country was stirred. They brought their sick and He healed them. It was a day of visitation. A divine Person was among them in mighty power. The light was shining in Galilee of the Gentiles, described by some as the most oppressed, the most corrupt, and the darkest province of those parts. It was the beginning of a miraculous ministry that would subdue sickness and dispel disease, a ministry that would calm the storm and even raise the dead. God was visiting them indeed. Where the word of a king is, there is power. Though unrecognised, the King had come.

The deep, the demons, and the dead,
Were subject to the word He said,
Revealing thus His power and might
To exercise His Godhead right.

In that early ministry there was ample evidence that Jesus was Messiah, and that He was God. These demonstrations of omnipotence were declarations of His deity. It was not to be wondered at that multitudes should come to Him. From all Galilee they came. They came from Decapolis, the ten cities of that region. They came from the south, from Jerusalem and from Judea. They crossed Jordan too, and came to Him from Gilead and from Perea.

Alas, it was not the glory of His Person that drew them to Him. It was the prospect of relief from their afflictions. They came, not to worship and adore, but to ask and to receive. In grace He met them and ministered healing to them. Bodies, minds, and souls, all felt the tenderness of His touch and the power and comfort of His word. The years of ministry had begun.

For the many months that were to follow Jesus would be the wearied, yet unwearying, Servant of Jehovah, tending to the needs of the vast crowds. He ever saw them as sheep without a shepherd and was moved compassionately towards them. They would make constant demands upon Him, so that the Son of Man would have nowhere to lay His head. By night, when the birds settled in their nests, or by day, when the foxes rested in their lairs, He would have little or no opportunity to rest. How many miles He was to travel. From village to village, from town to town, from province to province, He would walk in a tireless service for men. By the seaside and on the mountainside, on the highway and in many a humble home, He would minister graciously, tenderly, powerfully, for the good of men and for the glory of God. He may indeed be King, but He is Jehovah's Servant too. Is it to be wondered at that Jehovah should say to us, "Behold my servant…in whom my soul delighteth" (Is 42.1)? Willingly and gladly our hearts respond to this exhortation and with joy we contemplate Christ – and worship!

> *O Lord, when we the path retrace*
> *Which Thou on earth hast trod,*
> *To man Thy wondrous love and grace,*
> *Thy faithfulness to God.*
>
> *Faithful amidst unfaithfulness,*
> *Midst darkness only light,*
> *Thou didst Thy Father's Name confess,*
> *And in His will delight.*

The Sermon on the Mount

There are seven mountain scenes in Mathew's Gospel. This is the second of them. For the first one, see the story of our Lord's temptation in chapter 4. Here, in chapter 5, Jesus ascends the mount which has become known as "The Mount of Beatitudes" to give that ministry which is commonly called "The Sermon on the Mount". There were, of course, other sermons delivered on other mountainsides, and indeed the very last public discourse in Matthew was given on the Mount of Olives. But when we speak of "The Sermon on the Mount", most will assume that we refer to this discourse, recorded for us in Matthew 5, 6, and 7.

At once, however, there appears to be a problem. Matthew says, "a mountain", but Luke says, "the plain" (Lk 6.17). Critics and cynics decide that there is a discrepancy, a contradiction, but every true believer knows that there cannot be. There are no discrepancies anywhere in our Bible. The explanation of this is simple. Luke's "plain" is simply "a level place". It was a level place on the mountain slope, where the multitude could gather before the Lord and hear His word. Matthew and Luke agree. It was a level place on the mountainside.

But though the multitudes are there, and listening, still the ministry is particularly addressed to the disciples. They are in the midst of, but distinct from, the crowd. The teaching that follows is especially for them. The saints are a separate company, left in the world, sent into the world, but not of the world, and not like the world. As another has said, "The world goes its way and I am not part of it" (JND).

The opening word of the discourse is "Blessed". What a sharp contrast is this to that last word of the Old Testament - "curse"! The old dispensation of law had revealed the true nature of man. God had put the best of men, the chosen race, on trial under law, and they had failed. There remained only the curse, and with this word our Old Testament comes to a sad close. Then, after four hundred silent years, Jesus came. He brought a new order of things, and in this, His first recorded public ministry, He begins with, "Blessed". There follow seven beatitudes which describe the expected character, and happiness, of the true children of the kingdom. Two more beatitudes pronounce blessing in the face of opposition and persecution.

Perhaps one of the most profitable, devotional ways to enjoy these first twelve lovely verses of this chapter is to see in them an unfolding of the character of the Saviour Himself. Once, as the God of Sinai, He had brought to that awful mount the tables of the law. It was a high standard that they demanded. Now He comes to another mount, having Himself lived out that law perfectly for thirty years in Nazareth. His ministry now is an advance on the demands of the law, as we shall see. It is the character of Christ personally, and it is the manner of life which is expected of those who are in His kingdom, whether now or in a future day.

The word "blessed" (Gk MAKARIOS) has the thought of happiness, serenity, tranquillity. God is the "Blessed God". To be so blessed in poverty, in mourning, in meekness, in persecution, is surely contrary to the thoughts of men. But this is the way of the kingdom. Happiness when there is adversity, serenity when there is hostility, tranquillity in all the varied circumstances of life and testimony, such was the character of the Master, and such should be the character of His disciples.

"Blessed are the poor in spirit". We are not to be poor-spirited, but poor in spirit. This is the opposite of pride. The truly poor in spirit will have no rich thoughts of self, will make no high claims, will demand no rights, but will rest in this assurance, that the kingdom of heaven is already theirs.

"Blessed are they that mourn". This is not alone the sorrow of bereavement or the grief of domestic problems and hardships. It is also the mourning of those who grieve over the havoc that sin has wrought. It is that sweet sadness that characterised the Lord Jesus Himself as He wept with men, and for men, and became known as "The Man of Sorrows". Such will inevitably and eventually be comforted.

"Blessed are the meek". Meekness has been defined as "excessive angerlessness". This is a cumbersome, but very apt, definition. Our Lord Jesus said, "I am meek" (Mt 11.29). Paul reminded the Corinthian believers of the meekness and gentleness of Christ (2 Cor 10.1). Like the poor in spirit, the meek can rest in this, that Jehovah has reserved an inheritance for them. The promise is that the meek spirit will be richly rewarded.

"Blessed are they which do hunger and thirst after righteousness". Hunger and thirst! How like our physical needs. Bread and water! Jesus said, "I am the bread of life", and He has, too, the water of life (Jn 6.35; 7.37). For those who truly hunger and thirst after Him there is enough and to spare. They shall be filled. They shall be abundantly satisfied (Ps 36.8).

"Blessed are the merciful". God is a God of mercy, merciful and gracious (Ex 34.6). Our Lord dispensed mercy on every hand. His people are expected to show mercy with cheerfulness (Rom 12.8). We need not expect to be shown mercy by others if we ourselves cannot be merciful.

"Blessed are the pure in heart". Without holiness shall no man see the Lord (Heb 12.14). But where there is purity of mind and heart, thought and motive, there will be corresponding revelations of God to that soul. We sing, "Without a cloud between", and when it is so there can be on-going visions of the beauties and glories of divine Persons. Sin, impurity, will rob the soul of such revelations of God.

"Blessed are the peacemakers". It is a great thing to keep the peace when things are already in harmony. It is a greater thing to make peace when there is dispute and discord. The supreme and blessed Peacemaker Himself made peace by the blood of His cross (Col 1.20). He desires that the same virtue may be seen in us.

"Blessed are they which are persecuted for righteousness sake". Such characteristics as those which have been described will doubtless evoke persecution from the perverse world. It was so with the Saviour and it will be so with those who follow Him.

"Blessed are ye, when men shall...persecute you...for my sake". Indeed the very trauma of being persecuted for Him is a cause for rejoicing. "Rejoice", He says, "for so persecuted they the prophets which were before you". Those who are persecuted for His sake and for righteous living are in the illustrious company of the prophets of old and of the Saviour Himself.

This then is the beginning of our Lord's ministry. There are a little more than one thousand words in Matthew's Gospel and over six hundred of these are the actual spoken words of the Lord Jesus. These are mostly contained in six discourses, of which this "Sermon on the Mount" is the first. Having spoken of the blessedness of the believer, our Lord now proceeds with the discourse, showing the transcendence of grace over law.

The disciples were to carry a heavy responsibility. They were to be the salt of the earth, preserving what was good in Israel. They were to be also the light of the world, bringing enlightenment to poor Gentiles. In their testimony they were to shine with a righteousness which would exceed the hypocritical self-righteousness of the scribes and Pharisees. These proud and arrogant men quoted the letter of the law but were ignorant of the spirit of the law. They paid external homage to the law but failed to understand its deeper import. Theirs was legality, not spirituality. There was an outward show of religion, but no inward sense of holiness or sin, and the disciples of Jesus must be better than this. Accordingly, our Lord will make six references to the law, saying, "It has been said...". He will then show that the requirements of grace surpass the demands of the law but fulfil the spirit of the law.

It is important to note that there was but one law. There were ceremonial, moral, civil, and judicial aspects of it, but there was one law. The believer has died to it, and so has been delivered from its demands and penalties, but in his life, under grace, he fulfils all that it demanded, and more. If the law required him to go a mile, he will go two miles. Upon this Jesus now expands as He continues His discourse. He had not come to destroy the law, but to fulfil it and then introduce something infinitely greater. He will have a spiritual people, who will, by reason of their spirituality, live better than those natural men to whom the law was first given. And so His commentary on the law begins.

Had the law said, "Thou shalt not kill"? And had it pronounced judgment upon the offender? True, but anger in the heart was, in fact, akin to murder. To nurture anger in the breast, and in that anger speak with contempt of one's brother, angrily calling him, "Raca", that is, fool, brainless, stupid, worthless, was the spirit of the murderer. The true child of the kingdom would rather hasten to be reconciled, and indeed would see such reconciliation as a necessary prerequisite to worship. It was essential to be so reconciled, and quickly. The prolonging of the enmity was a sure pathway to disaster and judgment.

Again, they had heard it said, "Thou shalt not commit adultery". This was the seventh commandment of the Decalogue. The breaking of it had been, and still is, the cause of untold misery in a myriad families. But before the actual physical act which transgressed the commandment, there was adultery already in the heart. Deal ruthlessly then with the offending thing, Jesus teaches. It would be better to lose even a hand or an eye, than for some fleshly desire to result in a damning situation. Let not impure desires and lusts become a trap and a snare, culminating in an adulterous relationship, with all the sad and tragic consequences.

Again, they had heard of the writing of divorcement. But divorce was not God's way. There had been concessions under the law because of the hardness of men's hearts and the weakness of the flesh (Mt 19.7-9). Grace would no longer recognise these concessions, but would revert to God's ideal. Marriage between the man and the woman was for life. Only death could break the bond. There was but one exception, fornication during the customary betrothal period, when there was already a husband-wife relationship, though not yet consummated (Mt 1.19-20). Unfaithfulness, unchastity, on the part of the betrothed may not at times be discovered until the marriage was to be consummated in physical union, but whenever it was revealed it was grounds for a putting away and an annulling of the arrangement. In any other circumstances the marriage of the divorced person was adultery. It is well known that this exception is found in Matthew's Gospel only. His is the essentially Jewish Gospel and only Jews would be familiar with the legally binding betrothal prior to the consummation of the marriage.

Again, they had heard commands about oaths and swearing. But the true child of the kingdom did not need to swear at all, neither by heaven, nor by earth, nor by the Holy City itself. The Christian's word is his bond. His whole manner of life should be characterised by a truthfulness and honesty which requires no oath to his word. He is transparent. Lying and falsehood are foreign to him. His "Yea" means "Yea", and his "Nay" means "Nay", and people will so recognise his integrity that his word is believed and accepted by all who know him, without an oath.

Yet again, they knew about the law of retribution: "An eye for an eye, and a tooth for a tooth". But this could be construed as cold revenge, and this was not the way under grace. Of the Master it was later to be written, "When he was reviled, (he) reviled not again" (1 Pet 2.23), and with His followers it must be the same. Grace does not seek retribution. Grace does not demand rights or seek redress. Grace will turn the other cheek when one cheek is smitten. Grace will go that second unasked for mile and will give up the outer garment with the body coat. Grace will never refuse the genuine, needy borrower.

Finally, they knew that it was said, "Thou shalt love thy neighbour, and hate thine enemy". But there was a better way. Even the despised publicans and the Gentiles loved those who loved them. There was no reward in that. If the disciples really wanted to bear a true likeness of their Father in heaven, they would love their enemies and return good for evil. The Father sends the sun and rain upon all without partiality. His sun rises upon the evil and the good alike. The just and the unjust together share the rain which He sends. To be truly like Him we must then be kind to all. There is nothing extraordinary, says our Lord, about loving our brethren only. The love of God reaches out to the unworthy and the unlovable, and the love of His people must be the same. Well might we pray as we sing –

> *O to be like Thee! full of compassion,*
> *Loving, forgiving, tender and kind;*
> *Helping the helpless, cheering the fainting,*
> *Seeking the wandering sinner to find.*
>
> *O to be like Thee! lowly in spirit,*
> *Holy and harmless, patient and brave;*
> *Meekly enduring cruel reproaches,*
> *Willing to suffer others to save.*

The Sermon on the Mount continues into the two chapters which follow. There are many other matters of faith and practice which have yet to be dealt with and the Saviour will address these matters in some detail, particularly for those who profess to follow Him and who would presume to be His disciples.

CHAPTER 6

The Sermon on the Mount (continued)

In the previous chapter our Lord has dealt mainly with the scribes, in that He has expounded upon the law with which the scribes, in particular, were so familiar. Now, in chapter 6, He will deal with the Pharisees and their hypocrisy. Their title describes them as "separatists", and no doubt some were sincere, as, for instance, Nicodemus, or Saul of Tarsus. But, in the main, they had a "holier-than-thou" disposition and they were hypocrites. They loved outward show and ceremony and the praise of men. Jesus condemns their hypocrisy in three spheres. They gave alms, they prayed, and they fasted. These were all, in themselves, good and commendable exercises, but were done with the wrong motives. They loved to be seen of men, these Pharisees. But that was their only reward.

Take heed in the matter of almsgiving, says the Lord Jesus. It is right that we should remember the needy and be ready to help them. Almsgiving is to be commended, but do it quietly and sincerely, before God, and not trumpeting your giving in the synagogue or in the street like the Pharisee. The Father will see in secret what you give, and what is done in secret with a right motive, He will in due time reward openly.

In the matter of prayer also, the disciples were not to be like these hypocrites. Nor were they to be like the heathen. The hypocritical Pharisees prayed standing in the synagogue or at the corners of the streets, to be seen by as many men as possible. The Pharisee in the parable of Luke 18 is perhaps an example. He "prayed thus with himself". But true prayer is a spiritual exercise and the spiritual man will bow in prayer in the privacy of his own room, communing with God in solitude. As for the heathen, they engaged in a worthless repetitive chanting. Repetition of requests is not at all forbidden. It was to the vain incantations of the heathen that our Lord referred. His disciples were not to pray like that.

Indeed, the Master could suggest to them a model prayer. They should come as children to a Father, saying, "Our Father". They should come as subjects to a Sovereign, saying, "Thy kingdom come". They should speak as servants to a Master, saying, "Thy will be done". They should be as dependants before a Beneficiary, saying, "Give us…our daily bread". They should be as debtors coming to a Creditor, saying, "Forgive us our debts". They should speak as pilgrims to a Guide, saying, "Lead us". And in it all they should sincerely and primarily desire His glory and not their own. How different to the proud Pharisees and to the heathen should the followers of the Saviour be.

This prayer was not, of course, to be used in the empty repetitive manner which our Lord has just condemned, and which is so prevalent in much of Christendom today. The Saviour never intended ritualistic repetition, but rather gave it to His disciples as an example. Their praying was to be characterised by this same brevity and beauty, this intimacy and dignity, this simplicity and sincerity. In this manner, and in a spirit of dependency, they should speak to their Father. It is a great privilege to be permitted to address God in simple childlike trust, and these are the guiding principles when we do so.

Then there was the question of fasting. The Pharisees, when fasting, were deliberately downcast in their countenances. They disfigured their faces. It was evident to all that they were fasting.

What holy men they were! They had to be seen to be fasting, but in being seen they had the only reward they could expect, the admiration of men. The spiritual man might at times abstain from food and from things legitimate, but not in that kind of religious ritual, that ceremonial manner. Rather, he would sometimes be so taken up with divine things that food could become almost an irrelevance. Fasting would not be a religious imposition, but simply a corollary of intense occupation with things spiritual. For such there may be no praise of men, but the Father would see, and would compensate accordingly.

In the matter of treasures, Matthew speaks of these more often than Mark, Luke, or John. As has been pointed out in an earlier chapter, he writes of treasures that are eternal, and of those that are temporal. Some treasures are moral, some are dispensational, and some are ministerial. The treasures of the wise men of the East in chapter 2 are the first of these to be mentioned. Here in chapter 6.19-20 are the next references. As the Saviour emphasises, earthly treasure is vulnerable to thieves, to moth, and to rust. Treasure in heaven is not so. It is surely prudent therefore to have our hearts in heaven and our treasure there also.

Worldly matters will inevitably call us. There are sights and sounds all around us which will make demands of us constantly, but it is good to have a single eye and a sincere motive. We cannot be in service to two masters. The believer should desire, and determine, to be wholeheartedly for God.

Now, if we are truly God's servants we may safely rely dependently upon Him for the meeting of our recurring needs. He feeds the birds of the air and He clothes the flower of the field. Why then are we, His children, so often so full of care about food and raiment. Not even Solomon, in all his glory, was clothed as gloriously as God clothes the lily. The birds neither sow nor reap, nor fill granaries, but they are provided for by Him who observes even the fall of a sparrow. This does not, of course, sanction or encourage a slothfulness which says,

"God will provide", and then sits back in idleness. The Saviour is rather giving us a safeguard against anxiety and worry. The herbage of the field belongs to but a day, and tomorrow is gone. If God so clothes the transient grass and the fading flower, and so cares for the birds, are His children not more excellent than they?

Let us rest then in this, that the Father knows and loves and cares. It is ours to trust. Let us live for Him today and not be anxious about tomorrow. Let us seek first the kingdom of God and His righteousness, and the sure promise is that all these other things will be added to us. The unbelieving man is ambitious, striving for treasure, for glory, for food, for raiment. The word to the believer is, "Be anxious for nothing" (Phil 4.6). "Casting all your care upon him; for he careth for you" (1 Pet 5.7). "My God shall supply all your need" (Phil 4.19).

> *Trust today, and leave tomorrow,*
> *Each day has enough of care;*
> *Therefore whatsoe'er thy burden,*
> *God will give thee strength to bear.*
> *He is faithful!*
> *Cast on Him thy every care.*

CHAPTER 7

The Sermon on the Mount (concluded)

Our Lord concludes the Sermon on the Mount with a parable. Two men are building. One is a wise builder who makes sure of a rock foundation. When the rains descend and the floods rise and the winds blow, his house withstands the storm. It is founded upon rock. The other man is foolish. He builds on sand. His house may have looked equally as good as the other. It may even have gone up more quickly, and perhaps it may not have been so costly. But when the winds and rains came and the storm beat upon that house, it fell, and great was the fall of it. So, says the Lord Jesus, everyone who hears these sayings of mine and obeys them, is like the man who builds upon rock. Those who hear and do not obey are like the man who builds on sand. Men are divided, wise and foolish, according to their attitude to Him and His teaching. How early in His ministry does the Saviour emphasise the importance of obedience to His Word. It is wise to obey. It is folly to disobey. It is the difference between rock and sand. This consideration ought to help us as we look at these concluding exhortations in His discourse on the mount.

We are exhorted that there are times and circumstances when we should not judge. It is not always right or prudent to be judgmental. We know that in the assembly judgment is sometimes necessary, and this is sad. Paul indeed rebukes the

Corinthians for failing to judge when they ought to have judged. However, the same Corinthians failed in another way, in that they were judging when they ought not to have been judging. They judged the apostle himself. Here our Lord is warning against that needless, carping criticism of others which can so often be associated with hypocrisy. Someone has said, "Search others for their virtues, thyself for thy vices". How often do we so readily detect the mote in a brother's eye and fail to notice the beam in our own eye. What troubles we might be spared if we would judge ourselves more ruthlessly and others more sparingly.

We must zealously guard our character and our testimony. This is holy and precious and we must not give it to be devoured by dogs or trampled by swine. We must so live as to give no occasion for just criticism by the world. Dogs and swine are unclean. Our characters are precious as pearls. Live in holiness. Do not be careless in your living. To give the world opportunity to accuse you of wrongdoing is indeed like casting your pearls before swine. There will, inevitably, be accusations which are unjust and unfounded. It was so even with the Saviour and with His apostles. But we must not give any opportunity for criticism and blame which is justly deserved because of unrighteousness in our lives.

Through it all we must continue in simple and sincere believing prayer. Ask, seek, knock, says the Saviour. To simple faith there will be a divine response. He will give us whatever is for our good. If we seek in His will we shall find, and He will gladly open when we knock. It gives the Father pleasure to have the trust of His children. If earthly fathers know how to give good things to their children, how much more our Father in heaven. He will never give stones and serpents when we ask for fish and bread.

In this final section of the Sermon on the Mount there are two gates, two ways, two destinies, two trees, and two builders. Our Lord is emphasising that there is a choice to be made and that men are divided. Three times in John's Gospel we read that there was a division among the people because of Him (Jn 7.43; 9.16; 10.19). Sometimes it was about who He was, sometimes it was over what He had said, and sometimes it was about what He had done. Men are responsible, we must decide, and our attitude to His Person, His Word, and His work, will determine our destiny. ᚔ

There is a strait gate and a narrow way of discipleship. It is not a popular way, and they are relatively few that find it, but it leads to life. The other gate is wide and the road broad. It is a crowded road, with much noise and bustle, and much to attract. It has ever been the way of the majority, searching for pleasures and for the satisfying of the flesh. But it ends in death and destruction.

Then there are the ever present false teachers, dressed as sheep but preying on the unsuspecting like ravening wolves. Their evil intent is to lure souls to the wide gate and the broad way. How shall we know such men? If they appear in sheep's clothing, how shall we recognise them for what they really are? "Ye shall know them by their fruits", says the Lord Jesus. Observe what they are producing by their teaching. Do men gather a bunch of grapes from thorns, or figs from thistles? The question needs no answer. There are good trees producing good fruit and there are worthless trees producing the bad. By this principle we can discern the worth of the true teacher. The others are false, and destined for ruin.

Does our Lord here envisage the growth of a great Christendom where such false teachers are at home? They say, "Lord, Lord". They profess His Name and purport to be His servants ministering in His Name. But how many there are in the pulpits of Christendom to whom He will eventually say, "I never knew you: depart from me". How many there are who profess His Name but deny His glories. They deny His deity. They query His virgin birth. They decry His unique Manhood. They doubt His miracles. They belittle His Word. They refuse

His sacrifice. They disbelieve His bodily resurrection, and His ascension, and His coming again. Yet, for some reason, they still wish to be recognised as His teachers! False prophets indeed, worthless trees producing bad fruits from their pernicious teaching.

So does the Lord Jesus conclude His discourse on the mount with the parable of the two builders. His word is of paramount importance. The storm will eventually come, and it is well to be founded securely upon the rock of His Word. His Word has authority and assurance. Is it any wonder that the listening crowds were astonished? They had never heard such authoritative teaching from the scribes. The scribes were not men of conviction. They lived in the shadow of fellow-scribes and Rabbis. They were conversant with the opinions of Rabbis past and present, and would quote these rather than give their own understanding of a matter. With the Saviour it was not so. He taught with conviction and with authority, and the people had never heard it quite like this before.

In the next chapter Jesus will descend from the mount with His disciples to a lower plane. This discourse has occupied them with high moral ground, but now they must come down to the wretchedness below. We live in a defiled and defiling world. His word is our safeguard and our guide in the moral darkness which surrounds us, and He will now demonstrate the power with which He can keep and preserve us as we seek to live for Him. Our constant prayer must surely be -

> *O guard my soul, Lord Jesus,*
> *O keep me close to Thee;*
> *And if I wander teach me*
> *Soon back to Thee to flee.*

CHAPTER 8

Early Miracles

"Where the word of a king is, there is power", said Solomon (Eccl 8.4). Jesus now comes down from the mount to embark upon a miraculous ministry which will demonstrate His power. They have been on the mountain, elevated for a while in a consideration of the lovely characteristics of the children of the kingdom, but down below there is sin and sadness, moral corruption and demonism. They must come down from the mount to the wretchedness of man below. There is leprosy and palsy, fever within and tempest without, and the King will move in grace among them. After His teaching, His touch. After His preaching, His power. Peter will look back and say, "Jesus of Nazareth, a man approved of God among you by miracles and wonders and signs, which God did by him in the midst of you" (Acts 2.22).

"And, behold, there came a leper". Luke the Doctor says that the man was "full of leprosy". He was leprous through and through. He was incurably hopeless and helpless. But he had heard of Jesus and he came humbly but confidently to the Saviour's feet. He pleaded earnestly, appealing to the Lord's ability to heal him. Jesus touched him. It was not a fleeting momentary touch. The word "touch" means, "to handle freely". The Saviour touches the untouchable. He handles the defiled limbs but Himself remains undefiled. The leper is cleansed and the law is satisfied as the man shows himself to the priest and offers the appropriate gift (Lev 14.2-4).

As they now enter Capernaum there comes a Roman centurion, a Gentile, with a plea for a sick slave. He seemed an honourable man, who, according to Luke, was highly respected by the local Jewish community, and who had indeed built them a synagogue. He pleads his unworthiness, but he knows all about authority and he pleads this too. He knows, as a centurion, that behind every command of his there was all the authority of Rome and of Caesar. He was a man under that authority. He reasons, therefore, that behind every command of Jesus there was, similarly, the authority of heaven and of God. "Speak the word only", he begs, and Jesus marvels. On two occasions only do we read that Jesus marvelled. He marvelled at the unbelief of the men of Nazareth (Mk 6.6). Here He marvels at the faith of a Gentile, and the power which had been manifested to Israel now reaches out beyond the favoured nation to this Roman centurion as the word is spoken and the sick servant is healed. So, says the Saviour, many will come from the East and from the West, from the remoteness of Gentiledom, to enjoy the things that Abraham, Isaac, and Jacob enjoy, and many of those who were, nationally and nominally, the children of the kingdom, will be shut out.

They come now to Peter's house. Peter's mother-in-law is ill, lying in a fever. He touched her hand and the fever left her and she arose and served Him and His disciples. Perhaps this was just a little picture, a foreshadowing, of what He would do with Israel. How He longed to touch that nation in its fever, to lift His people out of their sad condition and see them engage in a ministry for God.

As the sun was setting over the Galilean hills the multitudes gathered to Him in that evening hour. They brought the sick, the diseased, and the demon possessed, and He healed them all. It was a fulfilment of Isaiah's prophecy in chapter 53.4: "Himself took our infirmities, and bare our sicknesses". He would suffer in true sympathy with them. He would share the burden of their griefs and their sorrows. He was, after all, on the way to Calvary where the sinful root cause of it all would be laid upon Him and He would suffer as a sin-bearer. But now, as daylight faded, He must take ship and cross the lake to the other side.

As He was about to leave them, a scribe appeals to Him saying, "Master, I will follow thee". Jesus answered him in words that have become immortal. "The foxes have holes, and the birds of the air have nests". By day and by night the creatures had their resting places. But while the foxes resorted to their lairs by day, and the birds went to their nests by night, the Son of Man had not where to lay His head. He did not have a settled home down here, and, in any case, wherever He went to rest, men sought Him and found Him, making constant demands upon Him. He truly had no resting-place. We cannot tell how this observation affected that scribe. Would he still follow?

Yet another came, apparently avowing that he too would follow. But not yet! He desired to wait until the death of his father. After that, and when he had attended to his father's burial, then he would follow. Not so, says Jesus, let the dead bury their dead. Let the materially minded attend to things material. You put Me first and follow Me. He must be Lord of all.

How much has been written of the storm that followed. A great tempest. The ship deluged in the waves. The fear of the disciples, experienced fishermen though they were. Then the tranquillity of the sleeping Saviour in the midst of it all. They wake Him. He gently rebukes their feeble faith and then rebukes the winds and waves. They obey Him, and there is a great calm. How He longs still to calm the storms in the lives of His people.

But now there is another storm. It rages in the breasts of two demoniacs living among the Gadarene tombs. The demon possessed man of Mark 5 and Luke 8 apparently had a deranged companion. There are two of them in Matthew's account of the miracle. They are fierce and dangerous men who make the road impassable for travellers, but they recognise the Son of God.

He casts the demon tormentors into a herd of swine. The storm is hushed in the lives of the demon possessed as the herd rushes down the steep slope to die in the blue waters of Galilee.

How sadly does this chapter end. They beg Jesus to depart out of their coasts. They prefer their swine. John Oxenham has so aptly put their plea into verse –

> *Rabbi, begone!*
> *Thy powers bring loss to us and ours,*
> *Our ways are not as Thine -*
> *Thou lovest men - we, swine!*
>
> *O get Thee gone, Omnipotence*
> *And take this fool of Thine!*
> *His soul? What care we for his soul?*
> *Since we have lost our swine!*
>
> *The Christ went sadly,*
> *He had wrought for them a sign*
> *Of love and tenderness divine -*
> *They wanted swine!*

As another has said, "The curtain falls upon the fairest sight in that countryside; a man at rest, robed by his Deliverer in a garment of righteousness and at last in his right mind". But Matthew, Mark, and Luke all alike record the sad detail that the Gadarenes besought Jesus to leave their coasts. They had no desire for the blessings He could bring. Has the heart of man changed since?

CHAPTER 9

Further Miracles

Half of the twenty miracles recorded in Matthew's Gospel are in chapters 8 and 9. The King was moving in power in the midst of a sad and sick humanity. It was not only power, there was compassion and tenderness too as He entered into human sorrow. He calmed their fevers, healed their leprosy, delivered from demonism, opened blind eyes, unstopped deaf ears, loosened the tongues of the dumb, and even raised the dead. For Israel it was Psalm 103.3: "Who healeth all thy diseases".

From the country of the Gadarenes the Saviour came back across the Sea of Galilee to Capernaum, which had now become "his own city". He had gone to live there after His rejection at Nazareth (Mt 4.13). What privileged cities these were. They were indeed seeing the powers of the world to come (Heb 6.5). They carried to Him, there at Capernaum, a man paralysed, sick of the palsy. Mark tells the story most graphically. The people thronged the entrance to the crowded house, but the friends of the sick man were not easily deterred. They ascended the outer stone staircase to the roof, broke up the tiling, and lowered their friend to the feet of the Saviour, who first pronounced forgiveness of the man's sins. Sin was a greater problem than palsy! He then challenged the hypocrisy and unbelief of the scribes. Which was easier to say, "Thy sins be forgiven thee", or, "Arise, and walk"? The former, of course, was easier to say, for who then could tell or see or know whether sins had been forgiven or not? "Arise, and walk" was a different matter. Men would wait and watch and know whether or not some power had been imparted to the paralysed man. There was power! The man arose at the Saviour's word. He departed to his house as the people marvelled and glorified God.

The call of Matthew follows. Of this we have spoken earlier, in the Introduction to these meditations. It was a simple call - "Follow me". There was an immediate, unquestioning response from the publican, "He arose, and followed him". Matthew is Levi. Little did he know, on that memorable day, that he, a poor despised publican, was to become the biographer of the King of Israel, and give to succeeding generations the first Gospel of the New Testament, the regal, royal, "Gospel according to Matthew". The young believer, and every believer, should take courage from this. Who can tell what God may have in mind for us when He calls us by His grace? Matthew prepared a meal for the Saviour and in bold testimony he invited many of his old associates, publicans and sinners, to meet his new Master and Lord. There were critics of course, but Jesus reminds them that it is the sick who need the physician, not those who are whole. These Pharisees had much to learn both about mercy and true righteousness.

The disciples of John the Baptist then had a problem about fasting. The disciples of Jesus apparently did not fast like John's disciples and the Pharisees. Why was this? It was not the time for fasting, Jesus explains. His disciples could not mourn while He was with them. But one day He would be taken from them, He would be rejected, and then, in the days of His rejection, His followers would deny themselves the pursuits and pleasures of the men of the earth. Then again, there was a new thing being introduced which would not mix with the ceremonial ritual of old Judaism. It would be like patching new cloth on an old garment, or like new wine poured into old skin bottles. It would never do. New wine must have new bottles. Jesus was bringing in a new order of things which would displace and replace and supersede Judaism. It would be entirely new. So much of the ritual which the Pharisees loved belonged to an old order, an era of law-keeping which was soon to pass away.

While He was explaining all this, Jairus came. He was a ruler of the synagogue. His little girl, twelve years of age, was dying, even now already dead. Would the Saviour come? Of course He would come. He arose with His disciples and followed after Jairus, but on His mission of mercy there was an interruption. A woman, whose very life had been haemorrhaging away since Jairus's daughter had been born, came near to touch Him. She had been ill for twelve years. Just as the little girl began to live, this poor woman began to die. Human physicians had failed her. She had spent all that she had. Her touch was a touch of faith upon the hem of the Saviour's garment. She touched and trusted! All His garments are fragrant with myrrh and aloes, and with the healing cassia (Ps 45.8). Jesus took time to speak words of comfort and assurance to the woman, who was instantly healed by her touch of faith. It was an interlude of grace, and the company then proceeded to the ruler's house and to the death-chamber.

The minstrels were there already, with their music and noise and professional wailing. He put them all out, mockers, mourners, minstrels and all. There is no room for earthly clamour when God is about to work. "The maid is not dead, but sleepeth", He told them, and they laughed Him to scorn. But with holy calm He takes the little maid by the hand, lifts her out from the grasp of death, and His fame is spread abroad.

Two blind men now follow Him imploringly. For a variety of reasons blindness has ever been a sad problem in Israel. "Son of David", the blind men cry, "have mercy on us". They follow Him into the house. He challenges them if they have faith in His ability to heal them, and in simplicity they answer, "Yea, Lord". As the woman had earlier touched Him, so now He touches them, and in accordance with their faith their eyes are opened.

Now there comes to Him a man dumb and demon possessed. How much demon possession there was in Galilee! When the demon was cast out the people marvelled, but still the Pharisees are critical. They blasphemously attribute His works to the Prince of demons. Later He will tell them that this blasphemy is the unpardonable sin (Mt 12.24-32). They attribute the work of God to the Devil. In a future day, when the man of sin is revealed, with his deceptions, men will attribute the work of the Devil to God. Oh the perversity of man in his unbelief!

Our Lord continues His busy ministry, travelling, preaching, teaching, healing, praying. Through cities and villages He moves in grace, teaching in their synagogues and ministering to their sick with compassion. "Moved with compassion" is, in the original text, one word. His whole being was moved emotionally, compassionately, as He saw the multitudes. As has been observed earlier in our meditations, in His teaching the Saviour expounded the message, in His preaching He applied it, and in healing He illustrated it. But while the harvest was great and plenteous, the labourers were few. It is still the same. "Pray", He urges. "Pray the Lord of the harvest that He would thrust forth labourers into His harvest". Note that it is His harvest, not ours. It is His prerogative to send. It is ours to hear His voice and move in obedience when and where He directs. It is a high privilege to be workers together, under God, in the gathering in of the lost and the gathering together of the saved.

In the chapter which follows the Master directs, empowers, and instructs the twelve, those first favoured preachers of the glad tidings.

CHAPTER 10

The Charge to the Twelve

Chapter 10 brings us to the second of the six great discourses of the Lord Jesus in Matthew's Gospel. This "Charge to the Twelve" is full of instruction on a variety of themes. There are forty-two verses of directions, encouragements, and warnings, for all who would serve Him, and while there is much which is of particular relevance to the twelve, there are, nevertheless, unchanging principles for His servants in any and every age.

Those who serve Him are the servants of sovereignty. It is the Lord of the harvest who calls and sends and empowers the true servant. What variety there was in this original band of twelve. How different the personalities as they were sent out two by two! How would the impetuous, impulsive Peter work in the harvest field with the cautious, melancholy Thomas? How would Matthew, the former tax collector for the hated Romans, labour side by side with Simon the erstwhile Jewish zealot? Only the grace that had called them could mould them, and equip them, and endow them with a compatibility to work together for Him.

The kingdom was at hand. The call to the work was urgent, but His servants were required to be sensitive about the call. They must indeed go at His command, to preach and give to men what He had given to them. But there were restrictions too. "Go not", He commands, "into the way of the Gentiles and Samaritans". The greatness of the need does not in itself constitute a call. It may truly be a cry for help, but the labourer must be sensitive to divine guidance in his response to the need.

They were to learn, too, a dependency which would trust Him to meet their every need. He would not send them warfaring at their own charge. They needed neither gold nor silver nor brass in their purses. Nor need they be anxious about food and clothing. He who cares for sparrows, and who feeds the ravens, and clothes the lilies, will care for His servants. He who was sending them out would provide.

In all their service they were to be characterised by a dignity which was worthy of the Master. They were not beggars. Nor were they canvassing. They were courteous ambassadors of peace. They must salute those who would receive them and leave those who rejected them, and in the Day of Judgment it would be more tolerable for Sodom and Gomorrha than for those who refused the ministry of these apostles and heralds of the Christ.

How wise and prudent they must be. He was sending them as sheep into the midst of wolves and they would need to be as wise as serpents. They were not to be cunning, of course, but watchful and wise, yet with the unalloyed simplicity and gentleness of the harmless dove. As wise as serpents they would detect the danger, and as swift as doves they would flee from it.

For these twelve, as for the remnant of a future day, there were warnings of persecution. They would be imprisoned and scourged. They would be arraigned before councils and synagogues and before governors and kings. They would be charged falsely and punished unjustly, but it was all for His sake and He would be with them in the trial. How literally was all this fulfilled in the twelve, and for that faithful preaching remnant after the rapture of the church it will be so again. But they must not fear. The Spirit of their Father would give them the right words for every occasion. Sadly, families would be divided, brother against brother, father against son, children against parents, even to causing the believing parent to be put to death. There would be universal hatred and persecution for His Name's sake, but their ultimate salvation was assured. It would be encouraging, though humbling, for them to remember, in the days of adversity, that as it was with them, so it had been with the Master. The servant was not greater than his Lord. If men called the Master "Beelzebub", what would they call His household? It was a diabolical slander both of Himself and of His disciples, but they must preach boldly and courageously. They had truth which must be made known.

The Saviour looks for loyalty in the midst of this adversity. He will confess those who confess Him, but will deny those who deny Him in their unbelief. He acknowledges that it will not be easy. It is a strange paradox, that the preaching of the gospel of peace and the presentation of the Prince of peace so often occasions strife among men. So, again, the Lord warns them of divided households. Sons, fathers, daughters, mothers, and daughters-in-law would be at variance. A man would not have to look beyond his own family circle for enemies. But love to Christ must prevail over family ties and earthly relationships. The heavy cross of loss of friends and companions must be taken up to follow the Saviour, and if that seemed like losing one's life, then so be it. In the reckoning of heaven it would actually be finding life, and keeping it eternally. We must get our priorities right.

The discourse is concluded with the encouraging reminder that all service and suffering is fellowship with Him. Whoever received them received Him, and this was a receiving of the Father too. In a coming day their faithfulness would be rewarded. Prophets and preachers and hearers alike would enjoy His "Well done". Even the little things done for Him would not be forgotten. A cup of cold water given in His Name would be appreciated and remembered. He would take notice of everything, and would suitably and appropriately recompense.

So the charge to the twelve is ended. It is a dispensational discourse with both a near and a distant application. The twelve were a remnant of Israel acknowledging Jesus as Messiah, and they would suffer for their testimony. Likewise there will be a remnant testimony in a day to come. That future remnant will find much instruction and help and comfort in the reading of this tenth chapter of Matthew's Gospel. Today we live and serve in an interim period, but there are abiding principles in the discourse which we can safely apply to our service also. There is a sovereignty which directs the servants. There must be a most necessary compatibility among the servants, and an urgency with sensitivity in the service. There is a call for dignity, courtesy, dependency, sagacity, simplicity, and loyalty. These great things should be the characteristics and portion of the servants of God in every age.

May we endeavour to be loyal and true servants, diligent in the great harvest field for the Lord of the harvest. May we sing sincerely -

> *Take my life and let it be*
> *Consecrated, Lord, to Thee;*
> *Take my moments and my days,*
> *Let them flow in ceaseless praise.*
>
> *Take my will and make it Thine,*
> *It shall be no longer mine.*
> *Take myself, and I will be*
> *Ever, only, all for Thee.*

CHAPTER 11

The Prophet in Prison

The charge to the twelve being concluded, our Lord now travels on to teach and preach in other cities, but John Baptist, the King's Ambassador, is in prison, and in some despondency. John has heard, in his imprisonment, of the mighty works that were being done by Jesus, and this creates a problem for him. Why, or how, should it be, that he, the King's herald, should languish in prison while others were apparently enjoying a ministry of deliverance? If Jesus really was the One who was to come why should His prophet be incarcerated in a prison cell? If others were being released from disease and deformity and demon possession, why should not he be released from his bonds? It seemed so rational to so wonder.

John sends two of his disciples to Jesus with a rather sad question. "Art Thou He that should come? Or are we to wait for another?" Was this indeed the same prophet who so recently had cried fearlessly, "This is He"? How boldly and confidently by the banks of Jordan had John pronounced Jesus to be the Messiah (Jn 1.30). How sadly does he now ask, "Art Thou He?". Poor John! Is he occupied with self and circumstances rather than with the Lord? Has this introverted occupation been the cause of his doubting? How often it is so with ourselves.

Jesus continues in a busy ministry before answering them. Compare Luke 7.20-22, where He seems almost to ignore their question for a little while. Then He turns to them, bidding them to go and tell John what things they had witnessed. The blind were seeing, the lame were walking, and the deaf were hearing. Lepers were being cleansed, the dead were being raised, and the poor were hearing the glad tidings. Then, a special, personal word for John: "Blessed is he, whosoever shall not be offended in me". John, prophet that he was, would have been familiar with such Scriptures as Isaiah 35.5-6 and other similar Messianic portions. The Saviour would have John occupied with that Word, and this in turn would occupy him with the Messiah. Occupation with the Scriptures and with Christ is better than occupation with self and circumstances. This was, and is, the antidote for doubting.

John's disciples having gone, Jesus now addresses the crowds concerning John. John was no reed blowing in the wind, He assures them. Neither was he just another prophet. He was the last of the prophets. He was that messenger of the Messiah who had been predicted in Malachi 3.1, who would prepare the way for the coming of the Christ. There was no one born of women greater than John Baptist. He was, if they had the sense to see it, that Elijah who was to come. As has already been remarked, in his dress, in his dwelling, in his diet, and in his deportment, he was indeed Elijah.

But the anomaly was this, that John had come announcing the kingdom for which they had been waiting, and yet they had opposed him. They had resisted him violently, which meant that those who would enter the kingdom must strive, equally violently, and strenuously make their way into the blessing. It was being opposed with violence. It must be entered with great resolution.

Having commended John, our Lord now turns to upbraid the people. They were an unbelieving generation in spite of all that they had witnessed. They reminded the Saviour of a scene in the market place, of sulking children who refused to respond to the calls of their companions. Some were playing at weddings, some at funerals, as children do, but there were some who would play at nothing. They would neither dance to the piping nor lament at the mourning. So John had come, with sombre notes of warning and of judgment, but they would not respond. Then Jesus had come, with sweet strains of love and grace, and still they would not respond. Of the austere John they said, "He has a demon". Of the meek and tender Jesus they complained that He was, "a friend of publicans and sinners". But wisdom is always justified by those that are wise, and in due time both Jesus and John would be vindicated.

The Saviour now turns to those privileged cities which had seen His mighty works around that north-west corner of the Sea of Galilee. He pronounces woes upon them. Chorazin! Bethsaida! Capernaum! Today there are only black ruins of all three. Those other three cities, Tyre and Sidon and Sodom would have repented if they had had the privilege of Chorazin, Bethsaida, and Capernaum. In the Day of Judgment it would be more tolerable for Sodom. These Galilean cities would perish. They would be brought down to hell for their unbelief. These were solemn words from a Saviour who was meek and lowly in heart.

It was a sad moment for the Lord Jesus. He was rejected by the unbelief even of His own city, Capernaum. But He turns from them to His Father and commences His brief prayer with thanksgiving. He could rest upon the love of His Father and the greatness of sovereignty. "O Father, Lord of heaven and earth…". If the wise and prudent of the world could not see these spiritual things, well, babes of faith in their simplicity would see and enjoy what the great ones of earth could not. It was a cause for thanksgiving. There was an essential unity and harmony between the Father and the Son. There was an intimacy in love and purpose, and it was the prerogative of the Son to reveal the Father to believing hearts.

The Saviour now turns back to the crowd. He extends that sweet and familiar invitation. How simple the vocabulary - "Come unto me". How sweeping the embrace - "All ye that labour and are heavy laden". How sincere the promise - "I will give you rest". Whether it is extended in a gospel context to burdened sinners, or whether, as some think, it is for the weary servants of the previous chapter, the invitation is equally precious, and to both, the promise is rest.

"Take my yoke upon you", He pleads. Service for Him is pleasant. His yoke is easy and His burden is light. There is rest for the sinner, rest for the saint, and rest for the servant. He is the best of Masters, meek and lowly, and He will surely and suitably reward all labour and toil that has been rendered for Him.

> *There is rest for the weary soul,*
> *There is rest in the Saviour's love;*
> *There is rest in the grace that has made me whole –*
> *That seeks out those that rove.*
>
> *There is rest in the blessed yoke,*
> *That knows no will but His;*
> *That learns, from His path and the words He spoke,*
> *What loving patience is.*

The King is Rejected

Chapter 12 is a crisis chapter in Matthew's Gospel. It is the chapter of the rejection of the King. Jesus presents Himself in a three-fold greatness, but the leaders of the nation hold a council to determine how they might destroy Him. He is, in the chapter, in His own words, greater than their temple, greater than Jonah, and greater than Solomon. The temple, with its priesthood, was their pride, but He was superior to their temple and their priests. Jonah was unique among the prophets, sent with a ministry to Gentiles, but Jesus was greater than Jonah and all their prophets. Solomon may have been their greatest king, but Jesus was greater than their greatest. Their priests, prophets and potentates were all eclipsed by Him, but in a stubborn short-sightedness they would reject Him. In the heart of the chapter the Lord speaks of Gentiles trusting in His Name. It was a quotation from Isaiah 42 and He was that Servant in whom the Gentiles would trust. His own nation would refuse Him. Gentiles would receive Him.

The critical Pharisees, in their hypocrisy, then reprove Him for the action of His disciples on that Sabbath day. As the disciples walked through the cornfield with Him they were plucking the ears of corn and eating them. As they would rub the ears of corn between their hands to remove the husks they were technically reaping and threshing! On the Sabbath! This was offensive to the legalistic ceremonialism of the Pharisees. But then, as the Saviour reminds them, even their King David had infringed ceremonial law when he ate of the shewbread in an hour of necessity, and, as well as this, the Son of Man was Lord of the Sabbath.

So then, since they had such scruples about Sabbath keeping, did they think that it was lawful for Jesus to heal a man on the Sabbath day? The Saviour asks, but He does not wait for their answer. What man among them would pitilessly, mercilessly, abandon some poor sheep fallen into a pit on the Sabbath day, and leave it there helpless until the Sabbath sun had set? Would not any man promptly lift the entrapped animal out, even on the Sabbath day? He heals the man with the withered hand and they forthwith plot His destruction. What perversity! What unbelief!

There follows the case of a wretched creature, blind and dumb and demon possessed. The Saviour heals him and the people are amazed. The Pharisees make the foolish observation that He casts out demons because of an association with Beelzebub the prince of demons. It was an absurd commentary. Could Satan be divided against himself? How could a divided household or kingdom stand? No, Jesus would bind the strong man and spoil his goods. He would deliver men from demon power, and these Pharisees were actually committing the unpardonable sin of blasphemy against the Holy Spirit. As the Saviour had earlier taught another man, one of themselves, a Pharisee named Nicodemus, only the Spirit of God could effect new spiritual birth in a man, and if a man blasphemously rejected the ministry of the Spirit this was a rejection of the only means of salvation. There could be no forgiveness for that man. Obviously, in this particular context the unpardonable sin could only be committed in that day of miracles, but the principle must still obtain that rejection of the gracious ministry of the Holy Spirit is a rejection of the only means of salvation. It is impossible to bring a man to repentance who has so despised that divine Person who alone can produce a work of grace in the heart of the sinner.

These Pharisees were guilty of gross wickedness and

inconsistency. They had an outward show of holiness, but it was only a veneer, a facade. They were a generation of vipers whose hearts were evil. How could they produce anything for God? How could a corrupt tree bring forth good fruit? How could hearts that treasured up evil produce anything but evil? The words that they spoke would condemn them. Could the people be expected to hear or trust such men? In the Day of Judgment all would be exposed, and judged accordingly.

The scribes and Pharisees then seek a sign! What blatant arrogance was this! After all His miracles of grace which they had witnessed, they ask for a sign! Jesus refers them to Jonah. As it had been with Jonah, buried for three days and then raised up with a ministry to Gentiles, so would it be with Him. Jonah their prophet had, in a figure, come back up from burial and had gone ministering to Gentiles, and it was Gentiles too who came with the Queen of Sheba to see their King Solomon. Gentiles would hear the message and see the glory of the Son of Man when He was risen from the dead. He would be preached among all nations. This sign of the prophet Jonah was the ultimate sign for an evil and adulterous generation. One day the men of Nineveh and the Queen of Sheba would testify against them, to their condemnation. A greater than Jonah and Solomon had been in their midst and they had refused Him.

How sadly would the last state of the house of Israel be worse than the first. Jesus had come, and in His gracious ministry He had, as it were, swept and garnished the house. He was expelling the unclean spirit, but it would return. They would reject the Christ who had come to them in His Father's Name, and they would one day receive an Antichrist who would come in his own name. That last state of the house would indeed be worse. This was a wicked generation.

While the Saviour so conversed with them, His mother and His brethren came, wishing to speak with Him. They told Him, "Thy mother and thy brethren stand without, desiring to speak with thee". "My mother?" "My brethren?" "Who is my mother?", He asks, "and who are my brethren?". Our Lord was not being disrespectful, but was simply showing them that natural ties and human relationships are not relevant in the kingdom. He beckons towards His disciples. "These are My mother and My brethren", He says. Those who would do the will of His Father were closer to Him than earthly relatives. There was a spiritual plane where there was something more important and more enduring than family and earthly friends.

At this crisis moment in the Gospel and in His ministry, our Lord will now leave the house and go to the seaside. It was a symbolic gesture. The sea is ever a picture of Gentile nations. He will leave the house and go to Gentiles since Israel will not have Him. Ultimately He will triumph. His kingdom will be a universal dominion as He reaps a harvest of souls from among the scattered nations of Gentiledom. But this is chapter 13. However, we sing as we anticipate -

> *I cannot tell how He will win the nations,*
> *How He will claim His earthly heritage,*
> *How satisfy the needs and aspirations*
> *Of East and West, of sinner and of sage.*
> *But this I know, all flesh shall see His glory,*
> *And He shall reap the harvest He has sown,*
> *And some glad day His sun shall shine in splendour*
> *When He, the Saviour, Saviour of the world, is known.*

CHAPTER 13

The Kingdom Parables

The opening words of this interesting chapter are most significant. "The same day went Jesus out of the house, and sat by the seaside". "The same day...out of the house...by the seaside". What an eventful day that had been. It was the day that the Pharisees had held council how to destroy Him. It was the day they had rejected Him in His three-fold greatness. It was the day they had blasphemed the Spirit of God and thereby committed the unpardonable sin. It was the day He announced a new relationship, greater than natural ties. On that day, He, in a figure, left the house of Israel and began a ministry by the sea, which is ever a symbol of Gentile nations. He went into a ship. He was physically out of reach of the multitudes, but they could hear His voice. All this is so aptly a picture of present conditions. The Saviour has gone into the heavens, out of reach, but His voice is yet heard, with a message of grace particularly relevant to Gentiles.

He will speak in parables, taking the familiar things of life to illustrate things spiritual. He later explains that He speaks to the people in parables so that only the sincere, exercised heart will appreciate the truths which He is presenting. To those who are willing to know, the parable will reveal the truth. For those who are not willing to learn, the parable will be but an interesting story, of no spiritual value.

Seven parables of the kingdom now follow, and an eighth parable which deals with the responsibility of those who presume to teach. We must not confuse the kingdom with the church. The church may indeed be in the kingdom but the kingdom is not the church. It is more extensive than the church and there are two lines of truth which must be distinguished. These seven parables will describe the course and character of the kingdom from the commencement of our Lord's ministry, and during His absence, and until He returns at the consummation of the age. It is the kingdom in a mystery form. Prophets who knew about a kingdom, and predicted it, had not envisaged a kingdom quite like this, with the King absent. Hence there are things "new and old". It will be shown that not everything in the kingdom is genuine, whereas, of course, everything in the church is. A kingdom is the domain of a king, but often in a kingdom there are subjects who are not truly subject. The kingdom of the heavens is the rule of the heavens, but there are those in that kingdom whose allegiance is feigned and nominal, and this will be judged.

The first parable, that of the sower and the seed, tells of opposition to the kingdom in a three-fold way. It is the work of those old enemies, the world, the flesh, and the devil. Some seed will fall on the hard-trodden wayside. The birds of the air snatch it away and there is no growth. Other seed will fall into shallow ground where there is promise, until the sun comes up and the scorched seed is withered. Again, some seed will fall among thorns, where it is choked. Jesus later explains to His disciples. The field is the world. The seed is the Word. It is the work of the wicked one to catch the seed away. With some persons there may be a fleshly, emotional response which does not endure. With others, the cares of the world or the deceitfulness of riches choke the Word. Rich and poor are alike vulnerable. But in spite of the opposition of the devil, the flesh, and the world, there is yet good seed which falls into good ground and bears fruit.

A second parable tells of tares being sown among the wheat. This is still opposition, but now in the form of imitation. The tares are "darnel", a poisonous grass which bears a resemblance to the true wheat. Our Lord later explains this parable also. While men have slept the enemy has been busy. Is it yet so in our own day? It is not our business, however, and indeed it is not possible for us, to purge the offending darnel out of the kingdom. The Lord of the harvest and His angels will attend to that at the end of the age. We may safely leave it.

Another parable now likens the kingdom to a grain of mustard seed sown in the field. There is a small beginning but phenomenal outward growth. How small indeed were those beginnings. A manger in Bethlehem. A carpenter's home in Nazareth. A few Galilean fishermen. A despised Jesus. An upper room. A cross and a tomb outside Jerusalem. What a great Christendom has grown from these! Birds of the air which would snatch away the good seed actually lodge in the branches of this great tree. The unclean birds are caged in a system of their own making (Rev 18.2).

There is yet another parable which portrays the outward growth of the kingdom. A woman kneads leaven into three measures of meal until the whole is leavened. No Jew would ever have understood leaven as a symbol of anything but evil. How soon did the leaven of evil doctrine corrupt the fine flour. Almost every aspect of Christ's Person and work has been corrupted somewhere in Christendom. His essential deity; His real and pure humanity; His virgin birth; His miracles; the meaning and virtue of His cross; His bodily resurrection; His visible ascension; the promise of His return; these have all been "leavened". These fundamental doctrines are today being downgraded, denied, and destroyed, in many a pulpit in Christendom.

But if all this seems discouraging, and causes us to wonder if there is anything good in the kingdom, yes, indeed, there are yet three more parables which will show that there is that which is real and genuine and precious to the Lord. There is treasure in the field. There is a goodly pearl to be purchased. There are good fish in the net. Look at Israel. There will yet be a remnant nation, His own peculiar treasure. Look at the church, a pearl of great price, for His glory. Look at the nations from which there will be those who, like the sheep of another parable in Matthew 25, will enjoy millennial bliss with Him. There is indeed a genuine thing in the kingdom in all these aspects, in Israel, in the church, and in the nations. There is always something for Him. In all things He must have the preeminence (Col 1.18).

Did the disciples understand all these things? They said that they did. Well then, they must be like diligent householders and bring out of their treasures things new and old. They would, of course, have knowledge of the things which had been taught by the Old Testament prophets and psalmists. But these twelve were now highly privileged men, recipients of a new revelation of things belonging to a new economy, a new order of things. The old things would need to be reiterated and restated. The new things would need to be explained and expounded, and this was their responsibility as those instructed in matters of the kingdom.

The parables are finished now. The people are amazed, as ever, at His wisdom. Is He not the carpenter's son? Are not the names of His mother, and His brothers and sisters, well known to them all? How does such an One do such mighty works and possess such knowledge? Their unbelief robs them, for His mighty works were limited there because of it. As He said, a prophet is not without honour except in his own country.

In chapter 14 the days will grow darker still with the murder of John Baptist, the King's faithful friend and forerunner.

Martyrdom, Multitudes, and Miracles

Dispensationally, we have arrived at a most interesting chapter. The King has been rejected, and in the previous chapter a mystery form of the kingdom has been announced. The parables there outline the course and character of the kingdom during the absence of the King. Now we have described for us the condition of things which will prevail during the days of the King's rejection, and this is pictured in the three incidents which comprise the chapter.

First we have the murder of John Baptist, an illustration of the persecution of the godly and of the testimony. This is followed by the miraculous feeding of the five thousand, a picture of blessing for the Gentile multitudes in this present age of grace. Then comes the storm, and an incident depicting the care of the Lord on high for His perplexed people in the troubled sea of life below.

The Herods were, perhaps without exception, evil men. They were puppet despots, their authority being conferred on them by Rome. This Herod is Herod the Tetrarch of Galilee, son of Herod the Great who massacred the innocents after the visit of the wise men from the East. He had imprisoned the faithful John who had dared to denounce his adulterous relationship with his brother Philip's wife. Now there is a feast in celebration of his birthday, with the customary indecencies. It is reminiscent of that other feast recorded in the first chapter of the Book of Esther, with the embarrassment of Queen Vashti. In the height of the revelry and dancing Herod made a rash promise, which, because of those present, he must keep. His troubled conscience told him that the thing was wrong, but he must save face, as they say, and so he gave the solemn edict. John Baptist was to be beheaded in his dungeon and the head of the faithful prophet was to be presented in a dish to the young dancer. An evil woman was the instigator of it all, cruelly and cunningly manipulating the circumstances. A king and a woman! Politics and religion! It has ever been so through the ages, until the alliance of priests and soldiers in the trial and death of Jesus, and the coalition of religious and civil authorities in the Acts of the Apostles. It will be so, too, until the scarlet woman rides the beast in the days of vengeance after the rapture of the church. Politics and religion are consistently joined in opposition to, and persecution of, the saints of God and their testimony.

As with the martyr Stephen in a later day, devout men attend to the burial of John's precious remains and then come to tell the King Himself. The Saviour's reaction is quiet and dignified. He departs in silence to a desert place, but His disciples and a great multitude follow Him. There might well have been a manifestation of justified anger, but instead we read of His compassion for the people and a gracious healing ministry.

It is now toward evening. The day is fading as the sun is setting. It seemed a reasonable suggestion of the disciples that He should send the multitude away. There was still time to buy victuals in the nearby villages before nightfall. Those were kindly words of the Saviour: "They need not depart". He would not send them away hungry. But the need was so great! It was beyond their ability to meet it, for their resources were meagre, five loaves and two fishes. John is very explicit in his record of the scene as he paints a background of human weakness. He was just "a lad", who had this provision, John says. They were "barley" loaves, which was a cheaper grain than wheat. The fishes were "small". A lad, with barley loaves and two small fishes!

The crowd numbered some five thousand men, besides women and children. They did indeed present a need much greater than the scant supply. But the King among them was Lord of land and sea. Little is much in His hand! He was greater than the need. He quietly took the bread and the fish, the harvest of land and sea, and He gave thanks and blessed the food. He then bade His disciples distribute to the multitude which was now seated on the grass by His command. They did all eat and were satisfied, and twelve full baskets of fragments remained after all had eaten. It is a fitting picture of this present age of grace. Twelve baskets remain for Israel after the great need of Gentile nations has been suitably met in the gospel. John writes that they would have made Him King there and then, but He retired to the mountainside to pray, apart and alone, and His disciples below, on the sea.

That night was a troubled night on the Sea of Galilee. The wind was contrary and the waves were boisterous, and the King was not with them. But He was watching from on high and in the fourth watch of the night, as the dawn approached, He came to them. He may indeed sometimes delay, as He did with the Bethany sisters in their hour of need (Jn 11.6), but eventually, in His own good time, He will come to succour His afflicted people. He walked on the sea. He put that which troubled them beneath His feet, but still they were afraid. Then those lovely words of comfort and cheer, which He would still speak to every troubled heart, "It is I; be not afraid". Peter still wanted assurance and Jesus said, "Come". Poor Peter! His courage failed him in the water, as indeed it was to fail him again in the moral storm of that last night of our Lord's trial before Caiaphas. An outstretched hand responded immediately to his cry for help and they came into the ship together, Peter and his Lord. The wind ceased. It is no wonder that they worshipped Him, and acknowledged, "Of a truth thou art the Son of God".

What a picture of this present day. How many saints are in a storm. How many are perplexed and afraid. But the Saviour knows. He still watches from on high, and the precious promise of the Psalm is, "He maketh the storm a calm, so that the waves thereof are still...so he bringeth them unto their desired haven" (Ps 107.29,30). One day, as the dawn breaks, He will come to us. The storms of life will be past forever and we shall enter in with Him to an eternal rest, and worship.

> *Jesus Saviour, pilot me*
> *Over life's tempestuous sea;*
> *Unknown waves before me roll,*
> *Hiding rocks and treacherous shoal;*
> *Chart and compass come from Thee:*
> *Jesus Saviour, pilot me.*

They came to the shore safely at the land of Gennesaret and the country was stirred with the news of His coming. They brought their sick and their diseased, seeking but to touch the hem of His garment, for just a touch brought health and healing.

The King's faithful ambassador was dead, but the King lives, and the miracles continue. Jesus will later come face to face with the Herod who murdered John, His friend and forerunner, but there will be no further message for that Herod. It will be a most telling and solemn sequel to the cruel murder of John Baptist, but that is another story, recorded only by Luke (23.9).

CHAPTER 15

Crumbs from the Table;
Bread in the Wilderness

The Lord Jesus detested, and repeatedly denounced, the
hypocrisy of the scribes and Pharisees. The disciples later
remark that He had offended the Pharisees, but no matter, the
King will judge hypocrisy wherever it may be found. Our
chapter begins with a religious criticism of the disciples for
eating with unwashed hands. It was a transgression of the
tradition of their elders. There was nothing in the Mosaic law
about such, but Judaism had an oral law which had been
committed to writing by the Rabbis and called "The Talmud".
This they reckoned to be not only equal to the written Mosaic
law, but actually superior to it. The Talmud contained endless,
sometimes ludicrous, additions to the law that was given to
Moses, and the Talmudic regulations regarding eating and
washing, and the manner and means of washing, were
complicated to say the least. The Saviour points out to them
that they, in a more serious way, transgressed the commandment
of God. They had chosen a clause in their Talmud which released
a man from the obligation of the well known fifth
commandment that a man must honour his father and his
mother. They might indeed have been offended, these scribes
and Pharisees, but they were hypocrites. They were blind
leaders of the blind, concerned with outward show and
neglecting the inner purity of the heart and mind.

The King leaves them. He travels north to the borders of Tyre and Sidon and is met by a distraught Canaanitish woman. What a contrast to the religious hypocrisy which He had just left in Jerusalem! The woman implores Him as the Son of David. Did she think that such an approach would somehow grant her favour? She had no rights in David, this Gentile woman, but the awful state of her demon-possessed daughter had brought her in faith to the feet of One whom she truly believed to be the Son of David, the Messiah. The Saviour, testing her faith, hides His grace momentarily. He was only sent, He says, to the lost sheep of the house of Israel. She worshipped Him. Her cry was compelling: "Lord, help me". Still Jesus will test her. She was an outsider and it was not right to take the children's bread and throw it to dogs. "Truth, Lord", she acknowledges, but argues that even those little dogs under the table eat of the crumbs which fall as the children eat. It was, like the faith of that centurion in Capernaum, greater faith than He had found in Israel. "O woman, great is thy faith", Jesus answers her, "be it unto thee", and in that very hour her daughter was healed. How such incidents as these must have cheered the heart of the Saviour, rejected by the hypocrisy of the scribes and Pharisees but received by the faith of a Canaanitish woman, just like that Samaritan outcast of Sychar in John 4.

Our Lord now travels south again, towards the Sea of Galilee. He went up into a hill by the lakeside and, as ever, the multitudes came. Well did Isaiah write, "The people that walked in darkness have seen a great light" (Is 9.2). It was the land of Zebulun and Naphtali. It was Galilee of the Gentiles, and the light was shining upon them. They brought their lame, their blind, their dumb, their maimed, and many others. They brought them right to His feet and in grace and power He healed them. What happy times were these! The multitude wondered, and glorified the God of Israel.

But now an earlier problem recurs. "I have compassion on

the multitude", He says. For three days they had been with Him, these throngs of people. They were hungry. It was, of course, the disciples who had the problem. Had they so soon forgotten what He had done before in similar circumstances? "Bread in the wilderness?", they exclaim, and such a multitude too! In reply to His question about their resources they say that they have seven loaves and a few small fishes. Again, as formerly, He commands the crowds to sit on the ground. The King will do everything in an orderly fashion. Besides, they needed rest as well as food. He still provides both rest and food for the obedient soul. "He maketh me to lie down in green pastures" (Ps 23.2).

He took the seven loaves and the fishes. He gave thanks. He broke them. He distributed to the disciples who in turn distributed to the waiting multitude. Four thousand men there were, beside women and children. They did all eat and were satisfied, and there were gathered up seven baskets full of fragments. There must be no waste. How dignified it all was, and how characteristic of the King Himself. How similar to the feeding of the five thousand.

It is important to note the references to the two miracles in the next chapter (16.9-10, and see also Mark 8.19-20). These references are important because there are critics of Holy Scripture who say that there was but one feeding of the multitude and that the writers of the Gospels have confused and duplicated the record of this miracle. In chapter 16, however, the Saviour Himself refers to two separate and distinct occasions. There were indeed five thousand fed, and there were four thousand similarly fed. That there were two miracles is confirmed by the Lord Jesus, to the confounding of the critics.

What is the significance of the seven loaves and the seven baskets, and of the three days that the people were with Him? All is perfection. In the study of Bible numerals the numbers "three" and "seven" both speak of completeness and perfection. The third day, too, might remind us of the resurrection day.

Jesus had proven completely and perfectly, during three years of miraculous ministry, that He was indeed the promised Messiah. The testimony to Israel had been absolute. One day, when the King returns to earth, there will be, in symbol, seven baskets, and twelve baskets, for Israel. The nation will enter into blessing, and into government. A risen and glorified Messiah will ensure the millennial blessing of the people whose scribes and elders once rejected and crucified Him.

The Saviour now dismisses the multitude and journeys to Magdala, by the lake shore. This was the village home of that woman whom He delivered from demon possession, and who, it seems, never then left Him, but followed Him right to Calvary and to the Garden Tomb (Lk 8.2; Jn 19.25; 20.1). Who has not heard of Mary Magdalene, Mary of Magdala? What days those were. Well do we sing -

> *Tell me the story of Jesus,*
> *Write on my heart every word.*
> *Tell me the story most precious,*
> *Sweetest that ever was heard.*
>
> *Tell of the years of His labour,*
> *Tell of the sorrows He bore.*
> *He was despised and afflicted,*
> *Homeless, rejected, and poor.*

As preachers often say, it is the sweetest story that ever fell on mortal ears! It is the old, old story of a Saviour's love and it has won the hearts of millions down the years.

CHAPTER 16

The Great Confession

The very heart of this chapter is concerned with Peter's great confession at Caesarea Philippi. In the midst of religious confusion on this southern slope of Mount Hermon, Simon boldly acknowledges his Lord to be the Son of the living God. But before the confession there is opposition.

The Pharisees and the Sadducees were religious rivals, constantly in dispute and at enmity with one another. There was no correspondence between the ritualism of the one and the rationalism of the other. But from time to time they formed a strange and unusual coalition in a common opposition to the Lord Jesus, and so it is here at the beginning of our chapter. Earlier in his Gospel Matthew records that they both came to John's baptism. John called them "offspring of vipers".

They now come tempting the Lord and desiring a sign. What arrogance and unbelief is this. After all the miraculous ministry, of which they must surely have known, they desire a sign! Jesus knows their hypocritical intent and He rebukes them. They can look at the sky, He says, evening and morning, and can predict the weather, but they are spiritually ignorant as to the signs of the times. As He had already told the Pharisees (Mt 12.38-41), the only sign for them now is the sign of Jonah the prophet. Jonah, in a figure brought back from the dead, preached to Gentiles in Nineveh and reaped a harvest of repentance and salvation. So would it be with the Saviour. These proud leaders of Israel would reject Him. They would live to see Him crucified and raised from the dead, and forgiveness of sins preached in

His Name to Jew and Gentile alike. He left them, and warned His disciples to beware of the leaven of both Pharisees and Sadducees. Their doctrines were evil. Alas, Phariseeism and Sadduceeism, ritualism, traditionalism, rationalism and liberalism, live on in great Christendom, so that true believers still need to hear that word, "Beware".

Jesus now arrives at Caesarea Philippi with His disciples, and it is most important, and interesting, to note this location. Caesarea Philippi had in earlier times been known as Banias. Strictly speaking, this should be Panias, the town having been named after the god Pan. To this day there may be seen a grotto where stood the image of Pan. There is still evidence, engraved in stone, of the worship of Pan in that place. Philip had enlarged and refurbished the town however, and had renamed it Caesarea. But there already was a Caesarea in the land, on the Mediterranean coast, so the new Caesarea had to be distinguished. What better way to honour Caesar and gratify one's own ego than by combining the two names, Caesar and Philip, and calling the town Caesarea Philippi? Not content with this, Philip also built a white marble temple there for the worship of the Emperor, who, it was believed, was a god, a divine person. As well as all this, it is recorded that there were perhaps no less than fourteen temples erected in that vicinity for the worship of Baal.

What confusion indeed! Pan, Caesar, and Baal, heathen deities with their temples, their shrines, their images and grottos! And it was just here, in the midst of all this, that the Saviour asked the question, "Whom do men say that I the Son of Man am?". What did they think of Him, those who worshipped these other gods? Some thought, as did Herod, with his troubled conscience, that He was John the Baptist, risen from the dead. Some, perhaps with a little knowledge of the Scriptures, thought that Elijah had come. Others thought, in line with certain Jewish legend, that He might be Jeremiah, come to make preparation for Messiah. Or had they seen the Saviour's tears and were these a reminder of that weeping prophet? Others did not attempt to be specific but simply thought that He was one of the prophets.

Now Jesus repeats the question, but this time it is addressed directly to the disciples. "But ye, who do ye say that I am?" (JND). What did they think of Him? Peter does not hesitate. "Thou art the Christ, the Son of the living God". There was indeed a Living God. Pan, Caesar, and Baal alike, were but lifeless deities. But Jesus was the Son of the Living God, and He was the Messiah. This was a revelation of the Father to the hearts of those who were willing to know, and Simon Peter was, accordingly, a blessed man. If the Father had so spoken to Peter, and He had, then the Son would speak to him also. It is perhaps well known that there is an interesting play upon words. Peter was Petros, a stone, a piece of rock, and he was now manifesting the character of that Rock of which, by faith, he was a part. Jesus was that Rock. He was the Christ, the Messiah, and upon this Rock He Himself would build His Church. The new Ecclesia, to be built upon One who was Petra, the Rock, would be unassailable and impregnable, so that nothing could ever prevail against it, not even the gates, the power, of Hades, the unseen world of spirits. The authority of heaven would be invested in Peter and his apostolic companions. It was not in the temple now, nor in their synagogues. The message of the forgiveness of sins would be committed to these lowly Galilean fishermen, not to Israel's scribes, priests, or Rabbis. Jesus now charges them that they should tell no man that He was the Christ. That day was over. The nation had had its opportunity and its day of visitation, and had refused Him. The little company must soon leave Mount Hermon for Golgotha.

The Saviour announces, in the clearest terms, His impending sufferings and death. The leaders of the nation would condemn Him. He would suffer many things of them, and be killed. But He would be raised again, out from among the dead, on the third day. Peter objected. He would not have such a thought. He rebukes the Master, and the Master in turn rebukes him.

There follows the appeal. It is a call to all those who would be His disciples. They must be prepared to lose their lives and follow Him. What would be the profit anyway, if a man were to gain the whole world and then lose all that he had, his life, his very soul. The encouragement to those who would follow Him was this, that one day there would be glory, and in that glory there would be suitable reward. Indeed, soon the Saviour would give them a preview of that glory. They would see, albeit in microcosm, the kingdom, and the Son of Man in regal splendour. He would take some of them up the mount to grant them this foregleam of the kingdom. It would be a sight that they would never forget. It would strengthen and encourage them for future service, indeed for suffering, for exile, and for martyrdom. Peter, recalling the event after many years, was to write, "(We) were eyewitnesses of his majesty" (2 Pet 1.16). They were to see the King in His beauty. It would be worth losing the transient, tinsel glory of this world, or life itself, to share in the surpassing glory of that world to come. The story of the transfiguration is recorded in the next chapter. Meantime we sing -

> *There in the glory we shall gather everyone;*
> *Loud in the glory raise the joyful song*
> *Unto Him that loved us, never ceasing praise be given,*
> *Sing we Hallelujah, to the Lord of Heaven.*
> *Jesus, Lord Jesus, praise and glory be to Thee,*
> *Jesus, Lord Jesus, we shall reign with Thee.*

CHAPTER 17

The Transfiguration

The Holy Mount! So Peter calls it some forty years later. He could never forget that day (or was it night?) when he and the brothers James and John had climbed the mount with the Master. They had left earth behind on a lower plane for a little while and they had been rewarded with a sight of glory which remained with them until the end of their lives. Was it Mount Tabor? Or was it Hermon? Tabor, less than two thousand feet, could hardly be described as "an high mountain". The majestic Hermon however, towered some ten thousand feet high, the highest mountain in the region. But whether Tabor or Hermon, it most certainly was "the holy mount", where the glory of the Saviour shone out beyond the guise of the Carpenter from Nazareth, where the face of the Man of Sorrows was as radiant as the sun, and where, Peter declares, "(We) were eyewitnesses of his majesty" (2 Pet 1.16).

Matthew and Mark say that it was after six days. Luke says that it was after eight days. There is no discrepancy. Luke includes the first and last days of that period. Matthew and Mark count the intervening days only.

These three privileged men were to be given, as the Saviour had promised, a preview of the kingdom (Mt 16.28). They were to see that kingdom in miniature, in microcosm, and the King Himself gloriously pre-eminent in the midst of all. His garments, the Galilean homespun of His humble humanity, became dazzling white, white and glistering, white as the light, white as snow. In holy dependency, Jesus had gone up the mountain to pray (Lk 9.28). Heaven rewards the dependent Man and His disciples with a foregleam of the glory that is yet to be His as Jehovah's anointed King. His countenance and His raiment shine in that glory. What encouragement and comfort was this. Dark Calvary lay ahead, and He knew it. His visage would be marred there, cruel men would gamble for His stained garments at the foot of His cross, and they would write above His head, "This is Jesus, the King of the Jews". But if the sorrows of Golgotha lay before Him now, then kingdom glory lay beyond Golgotha, and it would be assurance for His disciples to know this.

As the glory shone, the heavenly visitors arrived, Moses and Elijah. It was fitting that Moses should be there. He was the founder, under God, of that economy which was soon to be done away. His types and shadows had foretold the Messiah, and were being fulfilled. It was fitting, too, that Elijah should be there. He was the great reformer and restorer of the nation, leading them back as Moses had led them out. They engaged in holy conversation with the King. Luke says that they talked of His exodus which He was about to accomplish. How well Moses knew the word "exodus"! The King's departure out of the world would be of His own arranging, whatever men may do or think. He was sovereign, and would order His own exodus.

Peter's Jewish mind desires to stay in the glory of the holy mount. He had objected to the prediction of the suffering of Christ, but this glory was different! It was good to be here. Poor Peter! He makes two blunders. First, it was not in the purpose of God that they should stay here. The Master was on His determined way to Jerusalem and to Calvary. It was not yet time for the glory. Second, and perhaps the more serious error, was in those words, "One for thee, and one for Moses, and one for Elias". Is the King to be on the same level as the law-giver and the prophet? But no! The heavenly ones must not stay. The law and the prophets must withdraw. Jesus must be left alone in solitary glory. A bright cloud overshadowed them, but this was no ordinary vapour cloud. It was doubtless the Shekinah. It was "the excellent glory", Peter says (2 Pet 1.17). The Father's voice came out of the cloud, reminiscent of that earlier day by the banks of Jordan, proclaiming, "This is my beloved Son, in whom I am well pleased". But for this occasion there is now an important addition, "Hear ye him". The Son would speak for the Father and would declare all the purpose of God. The King must be supreme. Hear Him! The fearful disciples fell on their faces before Him. In kindness He touched them and when they lifted up their eyes they saw no man save Jesus only.

Now they must come down from the mount, but they were not to preach or tell what they had seen. Not yet. The nation had already rejected the King. He was on His way to Calvary to die, and the preaching of His Messiahship was finished now. He had told them so at Caesarea Philippi (Mt 16.20). For those who would accept it, Elijah, of whom the scribes talked, had come to them in the ministry of John Baptist, and he had been rejected. The disciples now understood, but, in the words of J N Darby, "it was all up with Israel". After His three years of gracious ministry among them the nation had failed to recognise Him as Messiah and His sojourn among them was now drawing to a close. But down below, in the valley, on the plain, there was a pressing need, and He would in grace go down to them, and minister to them in spite of their unbelief.

A distraught father brings his demon possessed boy to Him through the multitude. "Lord, have mercy on my son", he pleads. The lad was in constant danger of fire and water, ever liable to be either burned or drowned. According to Luke he was an only-begotten son, this boy (Lk 9.38). How the heart of that Blessed Only Begotten went out to him! The King does what His disciples could not do. In their lack of faith, the disciples had not been able to help the poor boy. "Bring him to me", the Saviour commands. Demons must obey Him, if not them in their little faith. He rebukes the demon and delivers the child, and the disciples ask, "Why could not we cast him out?". "Unbelief", Jesus answered. If only there was genuine faith, He tells them, nothing would be impossible. While still in Galilee, He again announces His pending sufferings, death, and resurrection. He would be betrayed and killed, and the third day would be raised again. Betrayed? Was Judas Iscariot listening?

There now follows, in Capernaum, the question of His paying tribute money. This was a voluntary Temple tax, an annual half-shekel. "Doth not your master pay tribute?" the receivers asked. "Yes", Peter assures them. But when Peter came into the house the Saviour anticipated him and asked the question, "What thinkest thou, Simon? Of whom do the kings of the earth take …tribute? Of their own children, or of strangers?". Peter knew that it was of strangers. "Then are the children free", said Jesus, but He would give no offence, nor undue cause for criticism. He directs Peter to go to the sea and cast a hook. He who on other occasions could fill their nets with fish now uses one single fish for His purpose. "Take up the fish that first cometh up", He tells Peter. It would have a coin in its mouth, He says. Peter was to give this coin to those who received the tribute money. It was enough to pay tribute for two persons. That closing expression in the chapter is very beautiful: "For me and thee". The Master, in grace and in kindness, associates Himself with His people in the littlest things of life, and makes provision even for the payment of His servant's taxes. King though He is, from His lofty position in glory He still takes kind notice of His saints on earth, with all their failings. He is just the same today as He was then. And we sing –

Yesterday, today, forever, Jesus is the same;
All may change but Jesus never; Glory to His Name.

CHAPTER 18

Precepts and Parables

Sometimes the Saviour spoke in parables. Sometimes He enacted them. The enactment is simply a parable in action and such we have here at the beginning of our chapter. The contents of the chapter are built around two questions. The first was a recurring question among the disciples, "Who is the greatest in the kingdom of heaven?". The second was Peter's personal question, "How oft shall my brother sin against me, and I forgive him? till seven times?". Had they but known it, the two questions were intimately connected, for true greatness was really a humility which would not hesitate to forgive indefinitely. But the Lord graciously and patiently answers each question in detail.

Notice how the chapter commences, "At the same time…". Literally it is, "In that hour". The Master had, in that hour, just demonstrated what true greatness really was. Though He was Sovereign over all and Lord of the Temple, He had just waived His rights and had conceded to pay tribute money. He could have resisted and justly refused, but, as He explained to Peter, "Lest we should offend them…", and in humility He had provided the tribute money for Himself and for Peter. This was greatness indeed. It was in that same hour that the disciples brought their query about greatness in the kingdom.

He called a little child. How easily and freely and unafraid the children went to Him. This, too, is a mark of greatness. How unlike the austere and unapproachable Pharisees He was. He set the little one in the midst of the disciples and taught them. It was not human nature for a man to be childlike, so there must be conversion to be fit for the kingdom. The child did not press rights, did not arrogantly push its way, did not harbour malice, and did not aspire to worldly greatness. So the children of the kingdom must humble themselves and become as this child in their midst. As for those little children who believed on Him, woe to that man who stumbled them. Here is assurance, if assurance were needed, that even little ones may believe on the Saviour. We must never discourage, or offend, or despise them in their simplicity.

Offences would surely come, but woe to that man by whom they came. It would be better for him that he were drowned in the depths of the sea with a heavy millstone about his neck. So, the Lord exhorts, if any man had a failing in any respect, a trait of character which would tend to give offence to any of these little ones, let him deal with it ruthlessly. Was it a quick tongue? A hasty temper? An impatient spirit? A jealous nature? A haughty attitude? Let him hasten to be rid of such from out of his life. It was better that he live without it than die with it. The Father in heaven took constant notice of these little ones. They were precious to Him and the Son of Man had come to save them. They were like little lambs, gone astray by nature, but meaning more to His shepherd heart than those ninety-nine other sophisticated men who did not appear to need Him.

The Lord now returns to the question of offences between brethren. There was a proper and spiritual procedure to be followed, and the initial purpose and desire should not be to assert rights but to gain the offending brother. "Go and tell him his fault between thee and him alone", the Saviour says. Keep the matter contained between the two, the offender and the offended. If the problem could be resolved thus, then happily that was the end of it. No others need to be involved. There was, however, the sad possibility that the offender would not hear or respond. Go back to him again then, taking one or two others to help face the difficulty. It is imperative that differences should be settled somehow, and soon, else there is the danger that they will become like a cancer in the assembly, spreading a malign influence among the saints. Sadly, though, the offending brother may still refuse to hear, even with the help and advice of those who have accompanied the brother who seeks reconciliation. In that case, it was now a matter for the assembly to judge. Then, if there was no suitable response to the assembly, there would be a regrettable disciplining of the offender and the gathered saints would be in accord with heaven in any spiritual and orderly judgment of the matter. Even where there may be apparent weakness, just a small company gathered to His Name and for His glory, the Lord would be in the midst of them and would be in agreement with their spiritual and scriptural decisions.

This now raised Peter's other question, "How often do I forgive my brother?". Perhaps Peter thought he was being magnanimous in suggesting seven times, but the Lord multiplies this by seventy. Four hundred and ninety times! It is not to be taken literally of course, as if we could then refuse to forgive the four hundred and ninety-first offence! Jesus is simply emphasising the extent and the importance of a large forgiving spirit among brethren.

In keeping with this He now expounds a parable. A certain king was taking account of his servants and there was brought to him a servant who owed him the great sum of ten thousand talents. The servant's wife, his children, and his property, must all be sold to pay the debt, but he pleaded pathetically for the king's patience and for time to pay. The king was moved with compassion and graciously cancelled the large debt. This servant however, had a fellow-servant who owed him a hundred pence. Although this may have been about three months' wages, it was, relatively speaking, a paltry sum. There was no comparison between what was owed to him and what had been forgiven him, but he callously demanded immediate payment of that hundred pence, actually taking his fellow by the throat, saying, "Pay me what thou owest". He would not listen to the pleas of his debtor, and had him cast into prison until such time as the debt would be paid.

But other servants were watching all this, and, greatly grieved, they recounted to their royal master what had happened. The king was justifiably angry. Here was ingratitude indeed, that one who had been forgiven so much should refuse to forgive so little. He who had been the subject of great compassion and pity had denied the same compassion and pity to his fellow. "Thou wicked servant", the king charged him. "I forgave thee all that debt, because thou desirest me: Shouldest thou not also have had compassion on thy fellowservant, even as I had pity on thee?" The king, in his anger, rescinded the earlier cancellation of the debt and had him delivered to the jailers, who, in all probability, would torment him until the debt was paid.

The lesson for us all is so obvious. Who can estimate how much we have been forgiven? Who can assess the greatness of the mountain of sins that have been blotted out, or the extent of the debt which has been cancelled? How amazing God's compassion – who can measure it? And yet! Is there not so often among us an unforgiving spirit which denies to others what has been so freely granted to us? This brings no pleasure to the Father. He forgave us when we were but poor sinners. The offenders envisaged here are our brethren, they are members of the same family and of the same body. We who have been forgiven so much, "Shouldest not thou also have...compassion on thy fellowservant?". "Be ye kind one to another, tenderhearted, forgiving one another, even as God for Christ's sake hath forgiven you" (Eph 4.32).

CHAPTER 19

The Return to Judea

Jesus now leaves Galilee, commencing His final journey to Judea, to Jerusalem, and to Calvary. In great and customary grace He makes time for the multitudes that follow Him and He heals their sick.

It must be conceded that the passage that now follows has been the subject of much controversy among great and godly men, yet there are important and abiding principles concerning marriage which must be agreed by all. It is important to note that the Pharisees who now approach the Saviour with their question have no real interest in His answer, nor would they have any willingness to learn from Him. They came "tempting" Him, asking, "Is it lawful for a man to put away his wife for every cause?". Their motives were not pure. They were seeking to involve Him in an ongoing debate, a dispute among the various Rabbinical schools concerning divorce. Among the Rabbis the differing opinions about the grounds for divorce were legion. On the one hand there were those who held strictly to the sanctity of the family and the married state, and who spoke with reverence of "the four mothers", Sarah, Rebekah, Leah, and Rachel. With such, divorce was a last and most regrettable resource. At the other extreme there were those who treated women and wives with a certain contempt and sanctioned divorce for the most trifling and ridiculous causes. It would not be at all profitable to enumerate these.

Our Lord Jesus, as He had done before in what is known as

"The Sermon on the Mount", directs the Pharisees, not to tradition or to Rabbinical opinion, or even to the Talmud, the accepted code of Jewish civil and canon law, but to the Scriptures. What an example He has given us when problems arise, that we should resort to the Word itself for answers to those problems. "Have ye not read?" He asks. The Creator, who at the beginning made them male and female and instituted the marriage state, purposed that the union of a man and his wife should be an indissoluble unity which constituted them one flesh. It was never envisaged that this divine arrangement for mankind should be disrupted by divorce.

But the Pharisees now have another question. If this was so, was the teaching of Jesus in conflict with that of Moses who commanded a writing of divorcement when a wife was put away? Moses never commanded divorce, He tolerated it because of the hardness of their hearts. He commanded the bill or letter of divorce for the safeguarding of the rights of a divorced wife, but from the beginning this never was the divine intention. Whoever therefore would put away his wife and marry another woman committed adultery. In the parallel passage in Mark 10.11-12, this is just how it reads, but it is well known that in Matthew's account there is added an exception clause which reads, "except it be for fornication". It is this clause which has occasioned difficulty for some.

The question must be asked, "Why does our Lord use the word 'fornication', as distinct from the word 'adultery'?". There must surely be some reason for Him to distinguish the two words in one sentence. Our Lord never gives consent to divorce for adultery. Fornication is not the same thing at all. It is to be noted that this clause is only in Matthew's Gospel, the Gospel with a distinctly Jewish readership in view. Jewish culture and marriage custom had a betrothal period before marriage which was not so among Gentiles. Others have written more fully on the subject, as Alfred Edersheim, who writes, "A distinction is made between betrothal and marriage". But, he continues,

"From the moment of her betrothal a woman was treated as if she were actually married. The union could not be dissolved except by regular divorce". Any unchastity on the part of the betrothed woman during this period was fornication. It was not adultery. Such fornication during the betrothal period, when it was discovered, whether before the wedding ceremony or at the consummation of the marriage, was justification for dissolving the marriage arrangement. This was the only ground for divorce - fornication, not adultery.

All this raises the question in the minds of the disciples as to the wisdom of entering into such a binding marriage relationship at all. But the Lord points out that while at times there may be various and valid reasons for celibacy, such a celibate state was not for all men. The union of man and woman, husband and wife, was after all, a divine institution.

It seems so fitting that immediately following all of this they bring little children to Him. It is well known that so often where there is divorce, the real casualties of the breaking up of the marriage are the children. They are frequently torn between father and mother, by love and loyalty to both, and left confused. Is not parenthood one of the blessings and privileges of marriage? It is a responsibility, too, to bring children into the world and then bring them to the Saviour. The disciples rebuke the parents but Jesus gently rebukes the disciples. "Suffer little children, and forbid them not, to come unto me", He says. Is there an implication that if they are not hindered, the children will themselves come to Him in simple trust, whereas many who are mature and wise in the world will never come? He lays His hands on the little ones and blesses them. He then continues His journey southward to Jerusalem and to the cross.

Then there is the sad story of a very rich young man, whose riches were unfortunately greater than his desire for Christ. He addressed Jesus as, "Good Master". "Why callest thou me good?" the Saviour asked, pointing out that there was none good but God. Of course those who know the truth concerning

Him, know that He is good, because He is God. With this young man there had apparently been an upright and honourable life, but if a man is not prepared to put Christ before all else, then he lacks the real treasure. After a brief conversation he went away sorrowful. The cost was too great for him. Mark says that Jesus, beholding him, loved him. Would the Master really have asked him to give up all? Or was this a divine testing of the reality of the man's desire for spiritual treasures? He failed the test. It was easier for a camel to go through the eye of a needle than for a rich man to enter the kingdom either with his riches or by means of his riches. Those who enter do so as poor men, with nothing to offer by way of merit. It is all of grace, and undeserved.

Peter, however, remarks to the Lord that he and his colleagues had forsaken all to follow Him. They had not been like that young man who had just gone away sorrowful. What recompense would they have for following Him? The Lord occupies them with coming glory. There would be a day of regeneration for Israel. The Son of Man would sit on the throne of His glory, and in that day they would share His glory with Him. They would sit on thrones too, sharing with Him in the administration of the kingdom. If they shared now in His rejection they would share then in His exaltation. They would be recompensed an hundredfold, and it would be worth it all. The principle is still the same, as expounded by Paul in 2 Timothy 2.11-12. What if we are called to suffer for Him? One day we shall reign with Him. Sufferings for Him now are temporary and transient. The glory which awaits us is abiding and eternal. It will indeed be worth it all.

CHAPTER 20

Service and Suffering

Chapter 20 is in four parts, the first of which is the longest, comprising the first sixteen verses, almost half of the chapter, and dealing with service in the vineyard. The second part is very brief, where, in three verses, 17-19, the Saviour foretells His sufferings and death, and His ultimate resurrection. There follows the third section, verses 20-29, in which the ambitious mother of James and John seeks places for her sons in the expected kingdom. Our Lord's reply is to explain that true greatness in the kingdom is not as it is in the world, and He also predicts for them a share in His sufferings. The chapter closes, verses 30-34, with the story of two blind men whose sight is miraculously restored. These thirty-four verses range from the vineyard to Calvary and to the kingdom. The King is here, in sovereignty in the vineyard, in suffering at the cross, and in miracle-working power in His kingdom.

It will be noticed that this parable of the labourers is a sequel to the Lord's last words at the close of the previous chapter. "Many that are first shall be last", He had said, "and the last shall be first". This is repeated at the end of the parable in verse 16 of chapter 20. There may be, as some suggest, a veiled reference here to the coming in of Gentiles at a later hour than the Jews, to whom the Gospel came first. However, the dominant thought in the parable is that the Lord of the vineyard is sovereign, and in His sovereignty He can reward His servants as He so desires. Peter had said, "Behold, we have forsaken all, and followed thee; what shall we have therefore?" (Mt 19.27). Would there be a special reward for this? The parable expounds the Lord's answer.

To those who are the first to be hired in his service the lord of the vineyard promises a penny a day, and this is agreed. But in the market place at the third hour, and again at the sixth and ninth hours, and even at the eleventh hour, he finds labourers who are idle and he hires them likewise. The evening hour having arrived, the labourers are called to receive payment for their labour. They present themselves, as directed, from the last to the first, from the eleventh hour labourers to those who had laboured from early morning, and, "they received every man a penny". To those who had laboured all the day, through the heat of the Eastern morning and afternoon, this seemed unjust, and there was murmuring. Those who had wrought but one hour had been made equal to those who had worked all day, and it did not seem fair. Their lord's answer is a blending of statements and questions. "Friend, I do thee no wrong". Had there not been an agreement for a penny? Take what was agreed and go. "Is it not lawful for me to do what I will with mine own? Is thine eye evil, because I am good?" So the last shall be first, and the first last.

What is the relevance to us in the principles outlined in this kingdom parable? Two great lessons, at least, are here. First, the Lord of the vineyard in which we labour has sovereign rights, which must not, dare not, be questioned by the labourers. He does what He wills, and He is neither accountable nor answerable to any man for what He does. Happy is that labourer today who serves in the consciousness of the sovereignty of the Lord of the harvest. Second, that servant who serves for the glory of the Lord will not labour with his eyes on a reward. He will serve in the joy of serving Him who has called him. If the Lord will reward His servants, as He has indeed promised, then this is still sovereignty, but it is sovereign grace, that He should reward us for doing what was just a pleasure to do for Him.

Much of our Lord's ministry to His disciples was given as they walked along the highway. It was perhaps the opportune time to talk with them privately. Now, along the way, He tells them again of His forthcoming crucifixion. Notice that travellers to Jerusalem always go "up to Jerusalem". Even when, geographically, it might appear that the way to the City is downward, from northern parts, still it is "up to Jerusalem". Apart from the fact that the City is more than two thousand feet above sea level, there may be an implication that there was a moral elevation in the City which was known as "The Holy City". "Whither the tribes go up, the tribes of the Lord" (Ps 122.4). "We go up to Jerusalem", the Saviour told them, and He alone knew all that Jerusalem held in store for Him. There would be betrayal, trial, condemnation, and death. There would be mockery, scourging, and crucifixion. Jews and Gentiles would unite in rejecting Him. But He would rise again on the third day. Of course the disciples could not, or would not, accept it. Peter had said on an earlier occasion when the Lord had made a similar announcement about His death, "Be it far from thee, Lord: this shall not be unto thee" (Mt 16.21-22). It was easier to think of glory. It was not at all comforting to think that He who was their Lord and Master, whom they had accompanied for these three years and more, should be taken from them in such a cruel manner as He was predicting.

There is a certain sadness, that then, at the very moment that the Saviour was speaking to them of His approaching betrayal and suffering, Salome, wife of Zebedee and mother of James and John, should approach Him with a request regarding her two sons. She desired places of honour for them at His right and left hand in His kingdom. There was something insensitive about it, that, almost in the very shadow of His cross, they should be thinking of place in the kingdom. "Ye know not what ye ask", says the Lord. Then He asks, "Are ye able to drink of the cup that I shall drink of, and to be baptised with the baptism that I am baptised with?". They reply, "We are able". Notice that it is the sons who answer Him. If the initial request came from their mother, does it not seem that James and John at least knew of it, if in fact they had not prompted her to ask for them?

They would indeed share in His suffering, Jesus tells them. Although there were aspects of His sufferings which would be His alone, in which no others could have a part, yet, in some respects, these disciples would suffer similarly to their Lord. They would be mocked, scourged, and imprisoned, and even put to death for His sake. "We are able", they had said, and it came to pass.

When the other disciples heard of the conversation they were indignant. Why? Were they really upset that such a thing should be asked at such a time? Or does it rather suggest that they, too, coveted the positions of honour to which the sons of Zebedee aspired? Were they angry that others were pre-empting them, stepping in before them? A little later, in the Upper Room, on our Lord's last evening with them, they would all be in dispute as to which of them was the greatest (Lk 22.24). In any case, positions in the kingdom were the prerogative of the Father alone.

It is now that the Lord takes the opportunity to teach them again what true greatness in the kingdom really is. Of course He had already tried to teach them this, when they had earlier enquired as to who was the greatest (Mt 18.1-4). They seemed to be almost constantly obsessed with this question of greatness. In the kingdom, Jesus explained, it was not the same as it was in the world. In the world men were ruthless, desiring, like the princes of the Gentiles, to exercise dominion and authority. Men of the world wanted position and place and sometimes would give anything, or do anything, to attain it. But with these who were His disciples it must not be so. It was a paradox, strange but true, that in the kingdom if a man wanted to be great then he must become little. If he wanted to be greatest then he must become least. If he wanted to be chief then he must become a servant. The truly great ones among them would be those who were willing to be ministers and servants, deacons and bondslaves. Even the Son of Man in the midst of them had become a servant, and in His humility He would be obedient to the extent of giving His life as a ransom for others. And He was the greatest!

> Would'st thou be chief?
> Then lowly serve;
> Would'st thou go up?
> Go down.
> But go as low as e'er you will,
> The Highest has been lower still.

They left Jericho now, with a great multitude following. Notice the alleged discrepancy here. Matthew says that it was "as they departed from Jericho", and Mark also says, "as he went out of Jericho" (Mk 10.46). Luke however, says, "as He was come nigh unto Jericho" (Lk 18.35). There is no discrepancy. Some answer the difficulty by suggesting that there were two different miracles, one coming into Jericho, and the other going out. Others think that the blind men called for mercy as the Lord and His disciples were approaching Jericho, but that the healing actually took place on the other side of the town as they were leaving. Perhaps the more likely explanation is that there were two Jerichos. There was an old Jericho and a new Roman town, just as today there are two Jerusalems and two Nazareths, old and new. If the miracle took place between the towns then both statements are true, going in to one and coming out of the other.

As to the fact that Matthew speaks of two blind men, whereas Mark and Luke speak of one, again there is no mistake and no discrepancy. There cannot be, in a record inspired of God. Note that neither Mark nor Luke say that there was only one blind man. As Matthew Henry quaintly remarks, "If there were two, there certainly was one"! Does this Gospel of the Kingdom by

Matthew speak of two because of the divided and blind condition of the nation of Israel? The blind men did then what Israel will do in a day to come. They confessed Jesus as the Son of David, and in compassion the Messiah restored their sight. The miracle united them in a glad vision of Him whom they now followed in the way. So will it be with Israel when the King comes.

> *Him every eye shall see*
> *When He appears;*
> *Bright will the glory be*
> *When He appears;*
> *Soon shall the trumpet speak,*
> *Each sleeping saint awake,*
> *And the glad morning break*
> *When He appears.*

In the chapter that follows the little company comes nearer to Jerusalem, and nearer to Calvary.

CHAPTER 21

The King, the Village, and the City

This chapter has the distinction of bringing to us the very first mention of Bethany in our Bible. In the heart of the chapter, at verse 17, we read of the Saviour that "He...went out of the city into Bethany; and he lodged there". This is very significant. As A C Gaebelein remarks, "We are now reaching the beginning of the end". The city of Jerusalem has no room for Him. It has its temple and its priests, its ceremony and its ritual, and it neither needs nor wants Him. Bethany is different. It may be but a dusty street or two and a few simple homes, but here they will receive Him and love Him and make room for Him. In this chapter our Lord's movements and ministry lie between Bethany and Jerusalem, between the village and the city.

The early verses portray a fulfilment of a beautiful prophecy of Zechariah. "Jerusalem: behold, thy King cometh unto thee: he is just, and having salvation; lowly, and riding upon an ass, and upon a colt the foal of an ass" (Zech 9.9). The King now draws near to the city with His disciples, in literal fulfilment of the prophecy. This is often referred to as "the triumphal entry", and such, in a sense, it was. The very acquisition of the ass with its colt was a miracle. They found them just where Jesus said they would find them. The Lord had need of them, and, without question, they were granted. The tender grace of the Lord has been noted here in that there were two animals, a mother with her foal, and the Saviour would not have them separated. Although He needed but one, He asked for "them". If it is argued that the pronoun is in italics twice in verse 2, yet in the two occurrences of it in verse 3 it is not italicised, and verse 7 confirms that the disciples did bring "the ass, and the colt". Note also our Lord's omniscience. He who knew just where that fish was, with the silver in its mouth (Mt 17.27), knew also that over yonder, in the nearby village, there was an ass tied, with its colt.

It was quite a remarkable scene on the Mount of Olives. They put their garments over the animals and strewed the path also with garments and with branches of trees. No costly rugs and carpeting for this King, but homespun garments and palm leaves to prepare His way. The King was in the midst of them as multitudes went before Him and multitudes followed after. "Hosanna!" they cried, "Blessed is he that cometh in the name of the Lord". It was Psalm 118. "Hosanna" means, "Save now". "Hosanna to the Son of David" was, at least for the moment, a public acknowledgement that He was both Saviour and King.

As the great procession approached Jerusalem the whole city was moved, asking, "Who is this?". The city of the great King did not recognise its King. Jerusalem had been troubled at His birth, when the question was, "Where is He that is born King?" (Mt 2.3). Now, thirty-three years later, the question is not "Where?", but "Who?". Note the answer, "This is Jesus the prophet of Nazareth of Galilee". "Jesus"! There was greatness in that Name, but a greatness which they did not fully understand and could not explain. "Nazareth"! The town of ill repute where He had lived for thirty years. "Can there any good thing come out of Nazareth?", Nathanael had asked (Jn 1.46). "Galilee"! The northern province despised by the more sophisticated Judeans.

Jesus enters the precincts of the temple. It was still called "the temple of God", but men had demeaned it and desecrated its courts. There were merchants and moneychangers, noisily bartering and bargaining, cheating and defrauding, shouting and arguing. They had made the sacred court a market place and a den of thieves. Now, for a second time, Jesus purged the temple, the first cleansing being at the beginning of His ministry (Jn 2.13-17). What a scene it must have been as the King, with royal authority, cast them out and overthrew their tables. Coins would spill all over the pavement, with men and animals in confusion. Then judgment is blended with mercy, when, having cast out the merchants, He graciously healed the blind and the lame who came to Him.

But the wonderful things that He did, and the accompanying "Hosannas" of the children, angered the chief priests and scribes. "Hearest thou what these say?", they asked. "Yea", He replied, "Have ye never read, Out of the mouth of babes and sucklings thou hast perfected praise?". It was, of course, a quotation from the eighth Psalm. They must have known it. The sword of the Word pierced and silenced them. They had no answer. He left them, and went out of the city. This was symbolic. He crossed the Kidron Valley and went over the Mount of Olives to Bethany. How He must have appreciated the welcome and the loving hospitality of Bethany. He lodged there. That dusty village now meant more to Him than all the pomp and splendour of great Jerusalem.

Next morning the Saviour returns from Bethany to the temple. On the way over the mount He was hungry. What grace! Though He was rich, He had become poor. He was King, proprietor of everything, but yet He is hungry. He observes a fig tree and looks for fruit. There was foliage, so there should have been fruit. The fig tree is not like other fruit trees, where first there are leaves, then bud and blossom, and then the autumnal fruit. With the fig tree, fruit and foliage develop together, and if there are leaves then there ought to be fruit. "But", says Matthew, there were "leaves only". The Lord pronounced judgment upon the tree, and presently it withered. Is this the only recorded miracle of judgment? There is a parable in the miracle. As J N Darby comments, "Israel in fact possessed all the outward forms of religion, and were zealous for the law and the ordinances, but they bore no fruit unto God". The withering of the fig tree was but a foreshadowing of the approaching judgment of the nation which professed so much but gave so little. Just forty years after the beginning of our Lord's ministry Jerusalem would be besieged and destroyed, razed to the ground by the Roman legions, and the temple burned with fire. They would pay a heavy price for their failure to recognise their Messiah and King.

The disciples marvelled at the miracle and were exhorted to have that faith which never doubted but ever received from God what was asked in His will. In the temple court the chief priests and elders question the Lord's authority to teach. "Who gave thee this authority?" they ask. He puts a proposition to them. If they will tell Him whether the ministry of John Baptist was from heaven or of men, then He will tell them about His authority for His ministry. They were in a difficulty, and they knew it. If they said, "From heaven", then He would ask, "Why did ye not then believe him?" If they said, "Of men", they feared the people, who held John to be a prophet. Weakly they replied, "We cannot tell". "Neither tell I you", Jesus answered. In their hypocrisy they could not tell. In His judgment of their hypocrisy, He would not tell. But He would give them another parable.

A certain man had two sons. When he requested of them that they should work that day in the vineyard, the first bluntly said, "I will not", but afterward repented and went. The second replied promptly, "I go, sir", but went not. "Which of them did the will of his father?", Jesus asked them. "The first", they answered correctly. It was just an illustration of the different ways in which John Baptist's hearers had responded to his ministry of righteousness. These proud and polished leaders of the nation professed righteousness, but it was profession only. Lip and life did not agree. They did not practise what they preached. The publicans and harlots, however, whom they despised, and who seemed by their lives to be denying obedience, were coming in repentance and yielding to the claims of righteousness. They were entering the kingdom before the unrepentant, self-righteous, priests and elders and scribes.

Then there was another parable. There was a householder, a vineyard, a winepress in anticipation of fruit, a watchtower to guard against intruders, husbandmen to labour in the vineyard; and the owner went away to a far country. When vintage time came he sent servants to receive the expected fruit. These servants were beaten and stoned, and another killed. More servants were sent, and they suffered similarly. Last of all he sent his son, thinking that surely they would reverence him. But they said, "This is the heir; come, let us kill him, and let us seize on his inheritance". They caught him, cast him out, and slew him. What would the lord of the vineyard do to those husbandmen? "He will miserably destroy those wicked men", they replied. The Saviour then used the sword of the Word again. "Did ye never read...?" He asked. How such a question would have humiliated and angered them. They? Chief priests and elders? They who knew the Scriptures better than any? Did they never read? What a question! He quotes Psalm 118 to them, the very Psalm from which the children had quoted when they had cried, "Hosanna". Now, from that Psalm, He reminds them of the stone which the builders rejected, which became, eventually, the head of the corner. The stone of the Psalm was the Son of the parable. They would reject Him, these builders of the nation, these leaders in charge of the vineyard, but He would yet be exalted. This would be the Lord's doing, marvellous in the eyes of His people.

Men had a choice to make. They could fall in contrition and repentance upon the stone, and be broken. It would not be a pleasant experience. It would be humbling in the extreme, to bow low and acknowledge sin and failure. But the alternative was fearful. On whomsoever the stone would fall, it would grind him to powder. God would most certainly judge those who rejected His Son. The chief priests and Pharisees rightly perceived that His parables spoke of them, and but for their fear of the people they would have arrested Him there and then. In the chapter that follows He has yet more parables for them. The thoughtful among them would doubtless perceive His mind in His parables. Whether Pharisees, Sadducees, or Herodians, He had words for each and all of them.

CHAPTER 22

Pharisees, Sadducees, and Herodians

After the parable of the early verses, this chapter is composed of questions from Pharisees, Sadducees and Herodians, with final questions directed to them from the Lord Himself. These questions and answers form the four parts of the chapter which follow the parable. The parable is similar, if not the same, and with different emphases, to the parable of Luke 14.16-24.

A certain king had made preparation for the marriage of his son. Invitations had been extended and arrangements had been made with a number of guests. When the wedding feast was ready, servants were sent out to bid those who had been invited that they should now come. An abrupt statement says, "They would not come". The response of the king is to send other servants to them to explain the preparation that had been made for the dinner. Oxen and fatlings had been killed and everything was ready. "Come unto the marriage", is the appeal of the second invitation. Some made light of it all, and went their usual ways. Others took the servants, abused them, and even slew them. The king was understandably angry. He sent his forces, destroyed the murderers, and burned their city. Once again his servants were sent out, this time to gather in from the highways as many as they could find, both good and bad, to furnish the wedding with guests.

The parable is, of course, dispensational. For centuries there had been a promise to Israel of a kingdom of the heavens, with all the blessing and joy which that would bring. A long line of prophets had heralded the great event and at the appointed time Messiah came. He extended the invitation to them, a privileged and chosen nation, but they rejected Him and His ministry of grace. There would have been a feast of good things for them if they had come, but they would not. Notice that now, when other servants are sent forth with the renewed invitation, there is mention of sacrifice and death. When the work of redemption had been accomplished, God again appealed to the nation by the preaching of the apostles in the early chapters of the Acts of the Apostles. This was longsuffering indeed, that such mercy should be extended to those who had rejected and crucified their Messiah, God's Son. Once again the invitation was spurned. They not only made light of it but murdered Stephen in Acts 7 and James in Acts 12, and there were other martyrs too (Acts 22.4; 26.10). This was not now just a simple refusal to come, it was a climax. God would deal judicially with those who had so rejected all that He had prepared for them, and eventually, as in the parable, He literally destroyed their city. The Saviour had predicted it and had wept over Jerusalem. The long siege of the city in AD70, and the awful events that took place during the siege, ended with its ultimate burning and destruction.

The invitation, however, must go forth again, this time to the highways, to the good and the bad, to whosoever will come. All things were ready. The house must be filled. If the Jew will not come, who was first bidden, then the Gentile must be invited. The Gospel of the grace of God will call them in and the wedding will be furnished with guests indeed. How grateful we who are Gentiles must be, that if the offer of grace is "to the Jew first", nevertheless it is "also to the Greek" (Rom 1.16). The judgment of God concerning sinners is that "there is no difference: For all have sinned" (Rom 3.22-23). Likewise the grace that reaches out to such declares also that "there is no difference between the Jew and the Greek: for the same Lord over all is rich unto all that call upon him" (Rom 10.12). There is no difference in guilt and there is no difference in grace. The invitation now goes out to all.

> *Call them in - the Jew, the Gentile;*
> *Bid the stranger to the feast;*
> *Call them in - the rich, the noble,*
> *From the highest to the least.*
> *Call them in - the weak, the weary,*
> *Laden with the doom of sin;*
> *Bid them come and rest in Jesus;*
> *He is waiting - Call them in.*

In considering what now follows it must be remembered that this is a kingdom parable. The Church is not in view, but the kingdom of the heavens, viewed here as a sphere of profession where not everything is genuine or real. As is often said, there are both professors and possessors in the kingdom. The king observes a man not wearing the provided wedding garment. Just as the prodigal was dressed in the best robe (Lk 15.22), so it seems that these guests from the highways were provided with garments so that they should be suitably attired for the king and the wedding. There was one, however, who for some reason did not wear the garment of the king's providing. So it is in the kingdom. There are those who robe themselves in their own morality, culture, respectability, or even religion. This is not acceptable dress. Only Christ will suitably cover a man for God's presence. As Paul writes, "And be found in him, not having mine own righteousness...but that which is through the faith of Christ, the righteousness which is of God" (Phil 3.9). The intruder is confronted by the king himself, and, speechless, is cast out.

A most strange and unusual coalition of Pharisees and Herodians now came to question the Lord. They really had very little in common, these Pharisees and Herodians, but they were allied now to oppose the Saviour. They asked Him about paying tribute to Caesar. Was it right, or not? Their approach and address to Him was hypocritical in the extreme. They eulogised His Person, His teaching, His integrity, and His impartiality. All that they said of Him was true, but they did not mean a word of it. It was all feigned. If they had really meant what they said of Him they would have believed Him and received Him. It was a subtle question. Tribute to Caesar? Had He given a negative answer they would very quickly have reported Him to the Roman authorities with a charge of insubjection, if not of sedition and conspiracy against Caesar. Had He given an affirmative, approving of paying tribute to the Roman Emperor, this would hardly have been acceptable to the people or in keeping with His Messianic claims. How would He answer?

He calls them hypocrites. He knows their hearts, their motives, and their intentions, and says, "Shew me the tribute money". Did they not realise that He was making them handle the coin? Did they quibble about paying tribute to Caesar? They were not averse to having and handling Caesar's money! The image on the coin was that of the Emperor and they admitted it. "Render therefore unto Caesar the things which are Caesar's; and unto God the things that are God's", He said. They marvelled, and left Him. Notice that there is no record anywhere in Scripture of our Lord Jesus ever handling money. When, on that last long night of His suffering they brought false accusations against Him, they never ever thought of charging Him with being what He was, or doing what He was doing, for mercenary reasons. In all the records of His life and ministry, nowhere does He ever handle money.

The Sadducees then came to Him with their question, men who denied the truth of resurrection. They described a most grotesque and unlikely situation of their own devising, concerning a woman who had been married during her lifetime to seven brothers. They were, of course, basing their hypothetical problem on Deuteronomy 25.5. If there was to be a resurrection, whose wife would this woman be in some supposed after-life? Were they now sniping at the Pharisees who believed in resurrection? The Lord disposes of them very quickly. They erred on two counts. They were ignorant both of the Scriptures and of the power of God. As He pointed out to them, in resurrection they neither marry, nor are given in marriage, but are as the angels of God. He who said, "I am the God of Abraham, and the God of Isaac, and the God of Jacob", was not the God of dead prophets and patriarchs. He was the God of the living. The crowds, listening, were astonished at His doctrine.

The Pharisees then took courage to come to Him again, having observed how He had silenced their bitter rivals, the Sadducees. This, of course, would have given them a certain satisfaction. They send one of their lawyers to Him with an old question, about which there had been many Pharisaical councils and debates: "Which is the greatest commandment?". The Saviour reduced the entire law to two commandments. Love to the Lord God with heart, soul, and mind, was the first and great commandment. But there was another, like to it, "Thou shalt love thy neighbour as thyself". The whole law hung on these two commandments, "Love the Lord thy God", and, "Love thy neighbour". Love is the fulfilling of the law.

Now while they are all gathered together, Pharisees, Sadducees, Herodians, and the multitude, Jesus will ask them a question, perhaps two! After all, He has patiently heard, and answered, their questions to Him. He has listened to them and now they must listen to Him. What do they think of Messiah, He asks them, "Whose son is He?". They answered immediately and correctly, "The Son of David". Now His second question to them, "How then doth David in spirit call him Lord?". He is quoting from the Messianic Psalm 110. "The Lord said unto my Lord". David calls his Son, "My Lord"! Can they explain? How can Messiah be both David's Son and David's Lord? The simplest believer in the Lord Jesus has no difficulty, but for the Pharisees, and for every Jew, and for all those who deny the Deity of Christ, there is a problem. They could not answer. Every true believer, however, knows that Jesus is both the Root and the Offspring of David (Rev 22.16). David might well have used the words of John Baptist, and said, "He that cometh after me is preferred before me: for he was before me" (Jn 1.15). When once it is believed and confessed that Jesus of Nazareth is Jehovah of Eternity, and that He is the promised Messiah, then there is no problem with our Lord's question. For those who will not acknowledge that Jesus is God, one of the eternal Triunity, then the question is unanswerable. He had silenced them, and from that day forth they refrained from putting any more questions to Him. But how His people delight to sing –

> *Thou art the Everlasting Word, the Father's only Son,*
> *God manifestly seen and heard, and heaven's beloved One.*

In the chapter which follows, our Lord will expose and condemn, ruthlessly and in detail, the hypocrisy of these religious leaders.

CHAPTER 23

Scribes, Pharisees, Hypocrites

This chapter is in three parts. In verses 1-12 the King speaks to the multitudes and to His disciples, warning them of the hypocrisy of the ecclesiastical leaders. In verses 13-33 He addresses these leaders directly, pronouncing eight "woes" upon them. The remaining verses 34-39 are a sad lament over the nation and over the city, as the King foresees their ultimate and inevitable desolation. This will then be developed in the following chapter.

These scribes and Pharisees had placed themselves in the seat of Moses the legislator. Their precepts were right and proper, but their practice was wrong. What they taught and demanded of the people was, in the main, quite correct, but they themselves were motivated in their practices by pride and hypocrisy. They loved to be seen of men. The phylacteries consisted of two strips of leather, to each of which was attached a small box containing certain quotations from the Torah, the law. One of these strips was wound around the head, with the box resting on the forehead. The other was bound around the arm. So was indicated that what a man thought, and what he did, was all in observation of the law of Moses. The Pharisees, however, wore phylacteries which were broader than those worn by other men to attract attention to their professed righteousness. Likewise, the borders of their garments were enlarged also. It was all to make them conspicuous. At the feasts, in the synagogues, and in the markets, socially, religiously, and commercially, they vied for the attention of men. They loved titles: Rabbi, Father, Master. They loved honours, offices, and distinctive garb, and they were ignorant of that rule of the kingdom, that he who would be great must be servant, and he who would be truly exalted must humble himself. The King Himself was the great Exemplar of this basic principle of His Kingdom. It should be noted that Phariseeism does not belong to one dispensation only. The leaven of the Pharisees has permeated ritualistic Christendom with its robes and titles, and the believer must ever beware of it. Seven times in the verses which follow the King says, "Woe unto you, scribes and Pharisees, hypocrites!", and once, in verse 16, He says, "Woe unto you, ye blind guides".

"Woe unto you, scribes and Pharisees, hypocrites!". The woes commence in verse 13. These men were the spiritual leaders of the nation, but, by their example and influence, they actually hindered the people whom they purported to help. Scribes who were so familiar with the letter of the law should have known its deeper spiritual and moral import, but they had turned their backs upon it and upon the light. Those who followed them were led astray, so that both the leaders and the led were being barred from the kingdom.

"Woe unto you, scribes and Pharisees, hypocrites!". With mercenary motives they preyed upon defenceless widows, seeking gifts in money or in kind, and looking for applause from vulnerable women. They visited such houses, pretending to be what they were not, making long prayers as evidence of their spirituality and knowledge. We must guard against such hypocrisy. It was obnoxious behaviour and would receive greater judgment.

"Woe unto you, scribes and Pharisees, hypocrites!". They would compass sea and land to make one proselyte. For what reason? The motive was utterly selfish, the building up of their own sect. Judaism was torn with sects, schisms, and schools, each Rabbi having his personal following of disciples. These Rabbis were both jealous and zealous, ever seeking converts to their own particular party. They would stop at nothing to make a convert, and, having made one, they would indoctrinate the proselyte and often make him worse than themselves.

"Woe unto you, ye blind guides". They were both fools and blind, these leaders. Had anyone ever dared to so indict or challenge them like this before? The Lord speaks of the gold of the temple and the gifts upon the altar. These hypocrites preferred the gold and the gift rather than the temple and the altar. They were guilty. They either could not, or would not, get their priorities right. The temple and the altar were symbols of heaven and the throne of God, and they were greater than the gold and the gifts associated with them.

"Woe unto you, scribes and Pharisees, hypocrites!". Again their priorities were wrong. They scrupulously attended to the paying of tithes even on the smallest of garden herbs, as mint, and anise, and cummin, but they neglected the weightier matters of the law, as justice, and mercy, and faith. They strained out gnats from their wine and drinking water, filtering out the unclean, and yet they would with impunity feast themselves on unclean camel meat. It was cant and hypocrisy indeed.

"Woe unto you, scribes and Pharisees, hypocrites!". Externally they had a self-righteousness which concealed from men the inner corruption of their minds and hearts. It was like cleansing the outside of cups and plates while ignoring the defilement inside. The hearts of these Pharisees were full of extortion and intemperance, while outwardly they gave the appearance and impression of holiness. Once again the King charges them with blindness.

"Woe unto you, scribes and Pharisees, hypocrites!". They were like whited sepulchres. Outwardly such tombs were often attractive, even beautiful, but within they were full of dead men's bones, unclean and corrupt. It was even so with the Pharisees, outwardly appearing righteous to men, but full of hypocrisy and iniquity within. The King knew their hearts.

"Woe unto you, scribes and Pharisees, hypocrites!". Here is

the concluding woe. They adorned and garnished the tombs of prophets and righteous men who had been killed by the fathers. "If we had been in the days of our fathers, we would not have been partakers with them", they said. But yet in saying this, they were admitting that they were indeed the children of those who had killed the prophets. They had inherited the character of their progenitors. They were a generation of vipers. How could they escape damnation?

In spite of all these indictments, God would yet send them prophets and wise men and scribes, but what their fathers did, they would do also. They would kill and crucify, scourge and persecute, and all this they did, in their own generation, beginning with Stephen in the early days of the Acts of the Apostles. They would be as guilty as the murderers of righteous Abel, and Zacharias who was slain between the temple and the altar. God would hold them responsible for the blood of the martyrs.

This chapter closes with the well-known sad lament of the rejected King: "O Jerusalem, Jerusalem...how often would I...and ye would not!". For three years the Saviour had presented Himself to them in gracious ministry. He had pleaded with them, "Come unto Me", but they would not come. He would have gathered them, protected them, sheltered them, as a hen covers her chickens with her wings. They knew the figure well; it had been used in the Book of Ruth and often in the Psalms - "the shadow of His wings". They were as vulnerable as chickens and in great danger. The fox would get them, but He had to say, "Ye would not". Their house would now be left unto them desolate.

One day it will be different. The King whom they rejected will return to be vindicated. A remnant nation will greet the King when He comes in power and in great glory. They will say in that day, "Blessed is he that cometh in the name of the Lord". What a contrast is this "Blessed" to the woes of the earlier verses. The King will come. He will then gather His people and become their shield and defender, and they will confess Him "wounded for our transgressions (and) bruised for our iniquities". But this will be a remnant people. So many in the apostate nation will have received a false Messiah coming in his own name. They will be branded with his mark and will worship his image, while others will patiently await the appearing of the true King and the promised Messiah. When He comes -

Every eye shall now behold Him
Robed in brightest majesty;
Those who set at naught and sold Him,
Pierced and nailed Him to the tree,
Deeply wailing,
Shall the true Messiah see.

The next chapter deals with some of the details of the coming days of tribulation and vengeance prior to the manifestation of the King in the day of His power.

CHAPTER 24

The Olivet Discourse

As the preceding chapter was very practical, so the chapter now before us is prophetical. This great discourse on the Mount of Olives extends throughout chapter 24 and to the end of chapter 25. The little company is sitting on the mount, looking over the Kidron Valley to the golden city shining in the sun. The sight is beautiful. It is not surprising that the disciples should remark upon the buildings of the temple, but the Lord predicts destruction. The great stones which they see would one day be thrown down, with not one left upon another. This prompts a three-fold question to Him from the disciples. They want to know when these things shall be, what shall be the sign of His coming, and of the end of the age. They speak, of course, of the end, or consummation, of the Jewish age. These disciples are a Jewish remnant and they enquire with Jewish minds. To import the Church and the present dispensation into this chapter is to invite confusion. Jesus answers accordingly in a discourse which will be of inestimable interest and value to a believing Jewish remnant of a later day, after the Rapture of the Church.

The first question, which concerns the destruction of Jerusalem, is not pursued here, but is dealt with in the parallel passage in Luke 21. The Saviour now projects their thoughts to that future day when a remnant, just like them, will bear testimony in the midst of great difficulties and persecution. There will be false Christs in that day, appealing to sensitive souls who long for a Messiah for their deliverance. How easy it will be for some to be deceived. There will be wars and rumours of wars, with nations and kingdoms rising against each other. War will eventually bring famine, for when men are fighting they are not sowing and reaping. Famine will result in pestilence and death, and accompanying earthquakes will add to the terrible trouble. All these are but the beginning of sorrows, the birth pangs of the nation. Note the correspondence of this part of the discourse with Revelation 6.

In those fearful days of tribulation the godly will suffer much. For their faith they will be betrayed and afflicted, hated and martyred. False prophets will arise to confuse and deceive the people, so making the testimony of the remnant the more difficult. Iniquity will abound in the moral decadence of a corrupt and lawless society. Sadly, the love of many will wax cold. Many, however, will endure to the end and will be saved out of it all. This is not the salvation of the soul. It is the physical, bodily salvation of those who have lived through all the trials and endured until the end of the tribulation period. Their final deliverance is assured.

Before that period ends the gospel of the kingdom will have been preached in all the world by that faithful remnant which will have been divinely preserved for that purpose. Compare Revelation 7.3-8. It is important to remember that there is but one gospel for every age. It is always the good news of salvation through faith in Christ. There are, though, different emphases on the message, in accordance with the particular context. The "gospel of the grace of God" is a most suitable emphasis for the message of this present age, when by that grace the glad news of salvation is being heralded to poor Gentiles everywhere. The "gospel of the kingdom" will, in that day, emphasise the truth that the King is coming, glad tidings indeed for those in suffering, and an incentive to believe the message in preparation for His appearing. In other circumstances Paul will speak of "my gospel", and of "the gospel of God", and "the gospel of...the glory", and in the Book of the Revelation we read of "the everlasting gospel", but the gospel is always Christ, with whatever emphasis and in whatever age.

In the midst of that seventieth week of Daniel's vision, as recorded in Daniel 9, during which these things will take place, the "abomination of desolation" will stand in Israel's Holy Place. This abomination would appear to be the idolatrous image of the beast of Revelation 13. It is a blasphemous usurping of the very place of God Himself, by one who sets himself up as God, demanding worship as though he is God (2 Thess 2.4). Believers are now exhorted to flee from Jerusalem and from Judea, the epicentre of all this trouble. Flight must be urgent. They must not linger, not even to collect or recover those treasured earthly possessions. How hard it will be for women carrying infants, whether in the arms or in the womb. Winter conditions or ceremonial regulations may increase the hardship, and they should therefore pray for guidance and for safe travel.

There will be, in those terrible days, much confusion, but they must close their ears to every rumour that Messiah had come. When He does come there will be no mistaking His coming. As lightning shining from one end of earth to the other, so will be the brightness of His coming, and in that day Israel will be as the carcase over which the eagles hover. The eagles represent those enemy nations which will be the agencies of God's judgment. They will encompass the land, enemies of each other and of Israel, in preparation for the final battle of Armageddon. Sun, moon, and stars, and the powers of the heavens, will be shaken. Whether these are literal convulsions of the heavenly bodies, or, as some think, the death throes of governmental authorities, both supreme and subordinate, they are evidences that the Son of Man is about to be manifested in great glory. His angels will come at His bidding, and they will gather His elect to safety from every corner of earth.

The nation of Israel is variously presented in Scripture under the symbolism of three trees, the Olive, the Vine, and the Fig . Israel as the Vine is Israel as God intended her to be in the past.

Sadly, she failed, and did not give Him the joy that He desired. Israel as the Olive tree is Israel as God intends her yet to be at the head of the nations in millennial days. She will then produce, as it were, oil for warmth and light, for refreshment and health. Israel as the Fig tree is Israel under judgment, set aside judicially in this present age. But the Saviour points out that the Fig tree will blossom again. Men should watch for the putting forth of the tender foliage and fruit, and while it is true in principle that no prophecy refers directly to this present mystery age, nevertheless it may be possible even now to see the foreshadowing of this national revival. It is the budding of new life for that nation, and this is very evident in these present momentous days of Israel's returning to the land.

"This generation shall not pass", our Lord says, "till all these things be fulfilled". The statement is difficult and there are varying interpretations. Some think that the word "generation" should be understood as meaning that race, that nation, that family, that seed which sprang from Abraham, a people who will abide and remain, preserved until all is fulfilled. Others think rather that the Lord is indicating that the generation which sees the beginnings of these awful happenings will also see the culmination. It will not, they say, be a long protracted, indefinite period, but will all take place in the lifetime of one generation.

Another thought is that no reader, or listener, need wonder at the prophecy of these catastrophic future events, for in AD70, at the siege and destruction of Jerusalem, all these things were witnessed, all were partially fulfilled. This was not at all the complete fulfilment, but, nevertheless, all those things which are predicted here were experienced by the people of AD70, and they were the generation which was then alive when our Lord was ministering. The generation to which He spoke had not passed when, less than forty years later, Jerusalem suffered in this way. It is apparently on record too, that believers of those fearful days literally obeyed the injunctions and warnings of this Olivet discourse, and that they actually fled from Jerusalem and from Judea, so that no Christian perished in the siege. What happened in AD70 was a dreadful precursor of the times predicted in this chapter, yet to be fulfilled. For intensity and magnitude of suffering these future troubles will be unparalleled. For Israel, in spite of all that she has suffered in AD70, and in the pogroms that have followed, the worst is yet to come.

Now neither men nor angels know the date when the Son of Man will come. As men in the days of Noah were taken unawares in their complacency, so will it be when the King comes. Two men in the field, two women at the mill, will suddenly be separated, one taken away in judgment and the other left for millennial blessing. This is not the Rapture. It is unwise even to apply the verses so, as many do in gospel preaching, for such an out-of-context application of these texts has sown the seeds of misinterpretation in the minds of many. Such misuse of the passage tends to confusion and hinders a proper understanding of the Word. To warn sinners of the awful separation of friends and families at the Rapture, there are other Scriptures which are directly relevant to that event.

Men are exhorted to watch diligently in that day. The coming of the Son of Man will be unexpected and many will be caught unprepared. Faithful and wise servants will therefore watch as they serve. Some, apostate Jews, evil and false shepherds of Judaism, will abandon hopes of His coming and turn to things material, carnal, and sensual, to their everlasting ruin. The Lord of the faithful servant will reward him, and in the context that reward will be a place of responsibility and rule in the kingdom. The unfaithful servants will have their portion with those that are lost, amid eternal weeping and gnashing of teeth.

This discourse, another "Sermon on the Mount", continues into chapter 25, a chapter of parables of particular relevance to that believing remnant of a day yet future, after the Rapture of the Church. Neither the Church, nor the Church era, is envisaged in this discourse, yet even now believers may sing as they anticipate the coming of the King in power and glory –

> *Lo! He comes with clouds descending,*
> *Once for guilty sinners slain;*
> *Thousand, thousand saints attending,*
> *Swell the triumph of His train;*
> *Hallelujah!*
> *Jesus comes, and comes to reign.*

CHAPTER 25

The Olivet Discourse (continued)

There is a rather unfortunate chapter division here. Chapter 25 continues the ministry of chapter 24 and both chapters should be read together in an unbroken sequence. Our Lord now introduces the well-known parable of the ten virgins. It must be conceded that many excellent expositors interpret the parable of the virgins as depicting profession, both real and false, in this present age of Church testimony. Such expositors believe that with verse 45 of chapter 24 a new section has commenced in the discourse, dealing with Christian profession rather than with the things relevant to Judaism and the remnant of the earlier verses. Those who reject this view see a consistent continuing theme right through the discourse, all to do with the days of tribulation subsequent to the Rapture.

The opening word of the chapter is important, and perhaps decisive – "Then". The question must be asked, "When?". The parable should be understood as looking forward to the coming of the King with His Bride. The virgins are not the Bride. The Bride is then already with the Bridegroom in the Father's house, and Bride and Bridegroom will come out together to lead the guests into the joy of the wedding feast. To explain in detail just how this agrees with Eastern custom and culture, and with Revelation 19, would be outside the scope of this meditation, but the correspondence with both is strikingly accurate. Indeed, although the interpretation does not depend upon it, some ancient manuscripts, as the Syrian Version and the Vulgate, actually have three additional words in the text, and read, "Ten virgins that having their torches, went forth to meet the bridegroom *and the bride*".

If it is accepted that there is a consistent theme in this discourse, then the wise virgins would represent that faithful believing remnant of tribulation days, and the foolish would represent those of the nation who, while having a form of godliness, have no spiritual reality. The lamps are an undoubted symbol of profession. The oil is a well-known symbol of the Holy Spirit. The coming of the Bridegroom with His Bride will reveal reality. The midnight cry, "Behold, the bridegroom cometh!" will be the great moment of truth. It is quite true, of course, that such mixture of wise and foolish, true and false, prevails today in the kingdom. To quote the late E W Rogers, he says of the parable that, "Its main principles apply throughout the whole of the period from the time the Lord returned to heaven till the time that He again comes back to earth. Its principles apply to us of the present calling; its principles will apply to the godly after the Church has been taken away". But this parable is essentially a warning and exhortation for those who wait for the Son of Man. Believers today wait for the Son of God, their Bridegroom and Saviour. "Son of Man" is a title associated with Israel and with judgment, rather than with the Bride, the Church.

There now follows another parable, and the connecting "For" of verse 14 seems to indicate that the earlier theme is being pursued. A man is travelling into a far country and he calls his servants together. He delivers to them five talents, two talents, and one talent respectively, according to each man's ability. Neither in their ability or in their capacity are they equal, but their master will require only faithfulness with what he has given them. He will not expect a return from five talents from the man to whom he gave two, neither will he expect a return from two talents from him with whom he left but one. Two servants then served wisely and diligently. "Well done!" is the commendation. He calls them good and faithful, and rewards them with further responsibility and the assurance of a share in the joy of their lord. The third servant however, buried his talent in the mud. This was not only a disappointment, but also an insult, to the master who had entrusted him with the talent. There was a great lack of respect for the master, and there was also sloth and neglect. He was an unprofitable servant, having neither love nor regard for the one who had trusted him, and he would be dealt with accordingly. This is the judgment of those in Israel, who, in the days subsequent to the Rapture, will presume to be what they are not. They will be judged on the ground which they have taken up and will be found to be unprofitable servants.

The concluding parable is based upon a scene with which our Lord's hearers would have been very familiar. Invariably in Israel, sheep and goats run together in one flock, but on occasions, such as the watering of the flock, they must be separated. I once asked an Arab shepherd as he divided his flock at the watering hole, "Since the sheep and goats seem to run together happily for most of the time, why do you separate them now?". He answered without hesitation, "They are different. They are a different nature. The goats would molest the sheep and would not allow them to drink in peace". A different nature indeed! Here, in the parable, the King has come and is seated upon the throne of His glory with His holy angels in attendance. The nations are gathered before Him to be judged. This is not the Great White Throne judgment of Revelation 20. That will be a judgment of the resurrected wicked dead. So, to distinguish the two judgment scenes, this of Matthew 25 is often referred to as "the judgment of the living nations".

The King is now about to set up His millennial kingdom. It will be a righteous kingdom into which only the righteous will enter, and the purpose of this judgment is to separate from the nations those who have responded to the message of the remnant, the gospel of the kingdom. He will separate men just like the separating of sheep and goats. Many Gentiles will have heard and believed that message, "A great multitude, which no man could number, of all nations, and kindreds, and people, and tongues" (Rev 7.9). They have washed their robes and made them white in the blood of the Lamb. Scattered among the nations, they have received and befriended the godly remnant of preachers and their attitude to them is accounted as their attitude to the King Himself. "Inasmuch as ye have done it unto one of the least of these my brethren, ye have done it unto me". Whatever men do to the preachers of the gospel of the kingdom, and their message, they do to the King.

To the sheep on His right hand the King says, "Come, ye blessed of my Father, inherit the kingdom prepared for you". To those on His left hand the word is solemn, "Depart from me, ye cursed, into everlasting fire, prepared for the devil and his angels". On the one hand, there is blessing and a prepared kingdom. On the other hand, it is cursing and a prepared punishment. "These shall go away into everlasting punishment: but the righteous into life eternal". The words "everlasting" and "eternal" are the same word (AIONIOS), appearing twice in this closing verse of the chapter. The word expresses eternity. Punishment and life are alike eternal. Those who deny eternal punishment must therefore deny eternal life, and must answer this question, "Admitting that the Saviour wanted to teach eternal punishment, in what other way could He have said it?". The original word is found nearly seventy times in our New Testament and it is used seven times of the punishment of the wicked. If this punishment is not eternal, then, to be consistent, neither is the life and happiness of the righteous, nor indeed, the very existence of God Himself, of whom the word is used twice (Rom 16.26; Heb 9.14). W E Vine quotes Cremer, who says, "Aionios excludes interruption and lays stress upon permanence and unchangeableness". He remarks that it should always be translated "eternal".

On this solemn note the Olivet discourse is concluded. The Passover is now approaching, and with it the last sad hours of the Saviour. The shadow of the cross is now looming large across His pathway. Gethsemane and the betrayal, the House of Caiaphas and Peter's denial of Him, Pilate's judgment hall and Herod's Palace with their blasphemy, mockery, and agony, and Calvary itself, are now almost upon Him. He knows all that lies before Him, but with firm step He will move resolutely towards the accomplishment of the will of His Father.

> *No unforeseen event*
> *E'er took Him by surprise;*
> *Toward the Cross with fixed intent*
> *He moved with open eyes.*

Already the chief priests and elders and scribes are plotting His death, but loving hearts are waiting for Him in Bethany. While some men will pour upon Him their venom and hatred and scorn, a woman of Bethany will anoint Him with a fragrance which will cling to His garments for the sad days and hours which are to follow. But that is the next chapter.

CHAPTER 26

The Anointing, the Upper Room, the Betrayal, and the Denial

"When Jesus had finished all these sayings …". So the chapter begins. The Saviour's discourses are ended, and now we are to be occupied with His last movements before Calvary. This sad but beautiful chapter begins in the house of Simon, in Bethany on the Mount of Olives. It wends its way through the Upper Room and the Garden of Gethsemane to the palace of the High Priest on the Mount Zion. With the Saviour, the reader crosses the Kidron Valley three times in the course of the chapter. There are several prominent personalities here, each of them playing a part for good or ill in these final events in the life of Jesus. We shall read of Simon the leper, of Mary of Bethany, of Judas Iscariot, of Peter and the sons of Zebedee, of Caiaphas, of the Chief Priests, Scribes and Elders. These, with others not specifically identified, were all involved in the events of those closing hours. These leaders of the nation, having already in principle rejected Him, now gather in council in the House of Caiaphas to plan His arrest and death. They wish to do this as quietly and as subtly as possible, and not on the feast day, fearing an uproar among the people.

There follows a delightful interlude in the sacred record: the immortal story of the woman in Bethany who anointed the Person of Christ with a fragrance that filled the house and must have lingered for days. Sixty years later John identifies the woman as Mary (Jn 12.3). She seemed to anticipate the Saviour's death and her precious spikenard was probably intended for the embalming of His holy body. But had this devoted woman learned also, as she had sat at His feet, that He would not only die, He would rise again? He would not need embalming! She would not, however, be denied the loving ministry that she had in mind for Him, and she would therefore pour her spikenard upon Him now. It was His, after all, reserved and preserved by her for the One whom she loved so intensely. Here, in Matthew's Gospel, she anoints the head of the King. In John's account it is His feet. There is no discrepancy. She anointed His whole Person, but Matthew, Mark, and John, will each record that which is best suited to his particular theme.

The disciples complain indignantly about "this waste". Waste indeed? Is this waste, to pour out love and affection upon the Son of God? How sad it was. How hurtful to Him, and what a slight to Mary, but the Saviour defends her. It was a beautiful thing that she did, He says, and it would remain an everlasting memorial and tribute to her when much else would be forgotten. So it has been as He said. Until this day, almost two thousand years later, those who love Him love to read, to tell, and to sing, the story of the woman who lavished her appreciation and devotion upon Him in a dark hour. It was a delightful extravagance of love.

Judas Iscariot is remembered too, but for a wholly different reason. Mary has freely given, but Judas will covenant for what he can get. He barters with the priests. What will they give him, what price, what reward, for betraying his Master to them? The highest bid he can get from them is just the price of a slave, thirty pieces of silver (Ex 21.32). The price is agreed and now he awaits an opportune moment for his treachery. Arrest in the actual privacy of the Upper Room would have been ideal for them. Is this why the Saviour concealed its location from them when sending out Peter and

John to make the necessary preparation? (Lk 22.7-14). Is this why Judas left during the evening? Did he now plan to bring the priests to that room?

In the Upper Room the Saviour announces His betrayal. Whether the disciples fully understood or not, He indicates the traitor and Judas leaves the room on his dastardly mission. Our Lord never trusted Judas, as David had once trusted the traitor Ahithophel. Compare Psalm 42.9 with John 13.18 where the words "in whom I trusted" are omitted. They share together what is often called "The Last Supper". It was this indeed. It was their last meal together and it was also the end of the ceremonial Passover. This was about to be fulfilled in the death of the Lamb of God, and was to be superseded by a simple supper of remembrance which He now institutes. A loaf and a cup would be the chosen emblems, symbolic memorials of His body given and His blood shed. That this supper was intended not only for those disciples who were with Him in the Upper Room, but for all those who would believe on Him during the days of His absence, is confirmed to us by Paul in his letter to the Corinthians (1 Cor 11.23-26). It is to be celebrated "till he come".

Having sung a hymn, most likely that closing Psalm of the Passover celebration, Psalm 118, they leave the Upper Room for the Mount of Olives and Gethsemane. He warns them that they will soon be scattered, like as a flock of sheep might be scattered, but Peter boldly avows that he will never be offended. He would die with his Master, he proclaims, sooner than deny Him. However, He who knows all things knows both the fact, and the time, of poor Peter's approaching denial.

The Garden of Gethsemane is shrouded in mystery. Even those privileged three, Peter, James and John, could not go all the way with Him. It was an agony that none could share and "he went a little further". Gethsemane means "The Olive Press", where the oil was crushed from the olives. As another has written –

Gethsemane, the Olive Press,
And why so named let angels guess!

Here, in an agony, our Lord anticipated the cross. He does not shrink from dying. He would be saved, not from death, but out of death (Heb 5.7, RV margin). But this was no ordinary death. He was to become the holy Sin-Bearer. The face of God would be hidden from Him. Darkness! Loneliness! Forsaken! There was no other way! With the thought of it all He was exceedingly sorrowful and very heavy. He fell on His face to the ground, praying, and while His disciples waited for Him, they slept. He came to them and said to Peter, "What, could ye not watch with me one hour?". The spirit was willing, He knew, but the flesh was weak, and Peter was soon to realise just how weak the flesh really was. Jesus went away again to pray, and came back to them a second time, only to find them asleep again. This time He left them sleeping. He went to engage in prayer the third time, saying the same sorrowful words and each time repeating, "Thy will be done".

His supplications finished, He now returned to them once more, and while they talked, Judas, who knew the place, arrived with a multitude. It is possible that they had been to the Upper Room and found it now empty. Judas would assume that they had gone across to Olivet, and he brought them there, to the familiar garden. They carried swords and staves. O the irony of it! Swords and staves to arrest the Prince of Peace! Did they think that He would fight? Judas called Him "Master", and He called Judas "Friend". The traitor stepped forward and kissed Him and the foul deed was done. Treachery indeed! They laid hold on Jesus. The impetuous Peter wielded the sword. It was courageous, but foolish. As others have remarked, Peter was a fisherman, not a swordsman, and he wounded a servant of the High Priest. The Lord reprimands Peter. This was not the way. Those who used the sword would perish by the sword. Jesus points out that if He but asked of His Father, twelve legions of angels would come at once to His assistance and defence, but how then would the Scriptures which predicted His sufferings and death be fulfilled. It must be.

The ribald crowd leaves the Mount of Olives for the Mount Zion, crossing back over the Kidron Valley. Peter followed afar off and then sat in the courtyard with the servants to see the end. In the High Priest's palace the chief priests and elders, with the council, arranged for the testimony of false witnesses against Jesus, to determine His death. The witnesses did not agree, although many came, willing to testify, until at last they found two in apparent agreement. Jesus had spoken of destroying their temple, they said, and of building it again in three days. It was, of course, a distortion of His ministry of some three years earlier, when in this way He had predicted His own death and resurrection (Jn 2.19-20). To this charge Jesus made no answer, until He was adjured by the High Priest. Such an adjuration demanded a response. He must say whether or not He was the Christ, the Son of God. He answered in the affirmative, telling them that one day they would see Him, the Son of Man, sitting at the right hand of power. He would come in glory, in the clouds of heaven. This was enough! It was blasphemy, they said, and they needed no further witnesses. He was guilty of death. Caiaphas rent his clothes. What a symbolic act, though he could not know it. He was signifying the end of the Levitical priesthood. There would indeed be two more High Priests after Caiaphas, but they would be formal, powerless figureheads, and then, AD70, the siege and destruction of Jerusalem and their temple, and the end of Judaism and the old order. They then buffeted and beat the Saviour. They spat on His face and mocked and derided Him. How calm He was in the midst of it all. What majesty! What dignity!

Meanwhile Peter is outside, sitting with the servants at a coal fire. He was challenged by a girl, who said, "Thou also wast with Jesus of Galilee". He denied, saying, "I know not what thou sayest". Later, in the porch, another maid saw him. She spoke, not to Peter, but to others who were there, "This fellow was also with Jesus of Nazareth". Again he denied, this time with an oath, saying, "I do not know the man". After a while there came yet another, who, speaking directly to Peter said, "Surely thou also art one of them; for thy speech bewrayeth thee". For the third time Peter denied, cursing and swearing, saying, "I know not the man". It is early morning and the cock crows! Poor Peter! He remembers the conversation of just a few hours earlier. How he had protested then that though all these others should be offended, yet he would never be. "Lord, I am ready to go with thee, both into prison, and to death" (Mk 14.29; Lk 22.33). He leaves the crowd, going out to be alone with his memories, his remorse and his tears. He wept bitterly. Jesus had told him, "I have prayed for thee, that thy faith fail not" (Lk 22.32). His faith did not fail, but his courage did. The man who had been singing in the Upper Room had been sleeping in the garden, and now he was swearing in the courtyard.

Is there not a warning here, regarding the believer's associations and company, and a caution also against complacency? Peter walked with them, stood with them, and then sat with them at the comfort of their fire while Jesus suffered. He failed to recognise the danger at the first challenge. A second one did not seem to alert him either. The third challenge came, and now it was too late. He yielded and lapsed. One day the Saviour would challenge him again, three times, at a similar fire on the shore of Lake Galilee. It would be a public restoration for the man who had failed. But that is another story, to be told by the beloved John (Jn 21.9-17).

CHAPTER 27

The Trial and Death
of the King

What an awful irony is this, that He who is King of Kings and Lord of Lords should be led, bound with cords, to be tried before a pagan Governor! Yet this is the story of this great chapter. With reverent footsteps we follow the King's pathway to the cross. The long night in the house of Caiaphas is over now. The morning has come. Israel's chief priests and elders bring their Messiah, their prisoner, to Pontius Pilate, their Roman lord. They have already reached a verdict. They have decided His guilt, and they desire His death, but they do not themselves have the right of execution. That must have the sanction of the Romans.

Judas Iscariot is full of remorse. Perhaps he did not think that it would come to this. Could Jesus not have eluded them, evaded them, escaped this? When Judas saw that his Master, whom he never calls Lord, was condemned, he returned to the priests and elders with the blood money. "I have sinned", he exclaims, "I have betrayed the innocent blood". But these leaders of the nation were arrogant and ruthless men. That was his problem, they retorted. He threw down the thirty pieces of silver and departed from them. Judas hanged himself at Aceldama on the slopes of the Valley of Hinnom just outside the south wall of Jerusalem. Yet even the hanging is not the whole story, for when either the branch or the rope broke he fell headlong and his body burst asunder in a dreadful sight (Acts 1.18). It was a fearful end for a privileged man who had become a traitor and an apostate.

It had been night when Judas left the Upper Room. It has been dark for him ever since. He lost both his silver and his soul, and the money bought a burying ground for aliens. It was all a fulfilment of Scripture. The quotation is from Zechariah 11.13. Since Jeremiah was the author of the more lengthy prophecies of both "Jeremiah" and "Lamentations", it is likely that his name was then used to describe the whole collection of those prophetic writings usually referred to as the Minor Prophets. In a similar way we speak of the Psalter as being "The Psalms of David", even though David in fact probably wrote less than half of them.

Jesus stood in calm dignity before Pilate as the Governor asked Him, "Art thou the King of the Jews?". Jesus answered in the affirmative, "Thou sayest". "It is as you have said". To the accusations of the chief priests and elders He answered nothing, and again, when Pilate asked Him if He had heard their witness, He answered nothing. "As a sheep before her shearers is dumb, so he openeth not his mouth" (Is 53.7). Pilate marvelled. He never ever had a prisoner before him like this Man. His wife dreams about it, and is troubled, and tells him so.

At Passover time there was a custom. Any prisoner, at the will of the people, could be set free. Pilate mentions the name of one Barabbas, an insurrectionist, a murderer, and a notable prisoner. Which of them would he release in accordance with the custom? Barabbas or Jesus? What a contrast it was. The name "Barabbas" means, "the son of the father". Which was it to be? Jesus, the true "Son of the Father" or Barabbas the murderer? At the instigation of the priests the people clamoured for the release of Barabbas. But what then would Pilate do with Jesus, called Christ? The answer came in a roar from the crowd, "Let him be crucified". Pilate protested but could prevail nothing. It was a weak and spineless Governor who washed his hands of it all, maintaining his innocence in this condemnation of a just Man, of whom he had said more than once, "I find no fault in him". Nevertheless, the apostles in prayer link Pilate with Herod and their rulers as being against Christ, in fulfilment of the second Psalm (Acts 4.27). Barabbas is released. Jesus is scourged. "Why, Pilate?", we might well ask. For what reason? Why scourged if innocent? He is then delivered to them to be crucified.

In the common hall the mockery gathers pace. They strip the Saviour of His clothing, then robe Him in scarlet, perhaps the cast-off faded tunic of some Roman soldier. They put a crown of thorns upon His holy head and a reed in His right hand. They bow the knee, and in derision acclaim Him King of the Jews, and spit on His face. Behold your King! Robe! Crown! Sceptre! Homage! Anointing! All in mockery of His kingship. They then smote Him on the head with the reed. Note the painful order. Had they smitten Him with the rod first, and then crowned His smitten head with thorns, that would have been suffering enough, but they put a crown of thorns on His head and then smote Him on His thorn-crowned head with the rod. What agony! What pain! The sharp thorns were beaten into His brow. After the mockery they put His own garments on Him again and led Him out to Golgotha to die. It was early. He would be crucified at the third hour, nine o'clock in the morning. Hanging on the cross His suffering would continue under the burning Eastern sun until the sixth hour, and then in the darkness until the ninth hour, three o'clock in the afternoon. All this after a long sleepless night at the house of Caiaphas.

It was a strange procession that made its way out to Calvary that morning, through Jerusalem's narrow streets and across the highway to the hill.

> *Beneath an Eastern sky,*
> *Amid a rabble cry,*
> *A Man went forth to die,*
> *For me!*
> *Thorn-crowned His lovely head,*
> *Blood–stained His every tread,*
> *Cross-laden, on He sped*
> *For me!*

They crucified Him. They gambled for His garments, unaware that they were fulfilling an ancient prophecy (Ps 22.18). They sat down to guard Him and they wrote above His head, "THIS IS JESUS THE KING OF THE JEWS". Matthew and Mark call it His accusation. Luke simply calls it a superscription. John calls it a title. The thieves at either side of Him railed on Him. Passers-by reviled Him. The rulers mocked Him. They derided His apparent helplessness. He who claimed to be the Son of God and who had saved others, why could He not now save Himself and come down from the cross? Then, for those three hours, the darkness hid Him from their view until it was rent by the awful cry, "My God, my God, why hast thou forsaken me?". They did not understand it. Some thought that He called for Elias, and touched His parched lips with a sponge filled with vinegar, the sour wine which was the common drink of the Roman soldiers. The rest said, "Let Him alone, let us see whether Elias will come to save Him". Another loud cry and He yielded up His spirit. The King was dead!

As the earth quaked the veil of the temple was rent, and the rocks were rent too. Graves were opened, and the bodies of sleeping saints arose, to appear in the Holy City after His resurrection. It was a dark afternoon of mystery and wonder. The centurion and his men were moved with fear. Women who had known Jesus, and loved Him, and had ministered to Him, stood afar off beholding. It looks as though they had never left the scene of His suffering. Had they indeed watched there for six hours, Salome and the Marys?

When the evening began to draw in, that man came, of whom it has been said that he accomplished his life's work in an afternoon - Joseph of Arimathaea. In his heart he had already acknowledged the greatness of Jesus the Nazarene. Was it the sight of the suffering One and the little remnant of the faithful who stood by the cross that finally brought him into the open? He was a rich man, but he became a beggar that day. He went to Pilate and begged the body of Jesus and Pilate granted him his request. With the help of his colleague Nicodemus –

> Gently they took Him down;
> Unfixed His hands and feet;
> Took from His head the thorny crown;
> Brought forth a winding sheet
>
> Spices most sweet they chose;
> Aloes they brought, and myrrh;
> Wrapped Him with these in linen clothes,
> Gave Him a sepulchre.

A new tomb. A clean linen cloth. A great stone. These tell the story of the burial of the Saviour. It was a rock-hewn tomb in a garden. Joseph gave it as a free-will offering. Did he realise that it was but a loan? That it was only being borrowed? For three days only it would be needed and it would then be returned to him. The interest on his loan would be that his name would be inscribed in each of the four Gospels, and that all those who loved the Saviour would love him too for his reverent handling of their Beloved on that dark day of the crucifixion. And the Marys watched!

However, the chief priests and the Pharisees are not content yet. They refer to our Lord as "that deceiver", and they remembered that which His disciples perhaps did not remember. They recalled that He had said that after three days He would rise again! They want the tomb well sealed, and secured with a guard. "Ye have a watch", Pilate says, "You have a guard". "Go your way", he tells them, and is there a certain irony, or fear, or premonition, in what he then adds, "Make it as sure as ye can"? How sure would that be? They made it sure, sealing the stone and setting a watch. A Roman seal and a military guard! Could these hold the Lord of Life and Glory? The next chapter gives the answer and today every evangelist rejoices to preach what those men feared, "He is risen from the dead!".

> *Death could not keep its prey,*
> *Jesus, my Saviour.*
> *He tore the bars away,*
> *Jesus, my Lord.*

The story of the empty tomb and the risen Saviour will be told in the chapter which follows.

CHAPTER 28

The Risen Master

The three days which followed the crucifixion were days of silent grief. The two Emmaus disciples later summed up the feelings of those days when they said, "We trusted that it had been he which should have redeemed Israel" (Lk 24.21). They spoke in the past tense, "We trusted". Their hopes had been shattered and their hearts were perplexed, but an empty tomb and a Risen Master are about to change things forever.

Matthew tells us that it was "in the end of the sabbath" that the women came to see the sepulchre, but the word "sabbath" here is a plural word, "sabbaths"! What does he mean? It had, of course, been a busy week, and as well as the usual weekly sabbath there had been several feasts with their associated sabbaths. Matthew may simply mean that those sabbaths were now past, that it was the end of the sabbaths of that holy week. But might there be more in his use of the plural? This empty tomb to which he now brings us spells the end of that old era of law and of sabbath-keeping. It was the dawning of the first day of the week and it was, too, the dawn of a new dispensation with a Christ risen from the dead and triumphant.

The happenings are stupendous. An earthquake! An angel of the Lord descends from heaven with countenance like lightning and garments glistening as white as snow. He rolls away the stone and sits upon it, as if to proclaim by his very presence and attitude the greatness of the triumph. How important it is to note that he does not roll away the stone to let the Saviour out. Jesus is already risen from the dead. He has already vacated the tomb. The stone is rolled away to let His people in to view the empty sepulchre. It is not surprising that the guards trembled and became like dead men. The angel exhorts the women not to be afraid. He knows, he says, that they seek Jesus the crucified One, but he assures them that "He is not here: for he is risen, as he said". The tomb is empty, but they may come, he invites, and see the place where the Lord lay. What news was this! Then, having viewed the empty tomb they must go quickly and tell His disciples. It was, as another has said, "Light after darkness: calm after storm: hope after despair: joy after grief". The great Shepherd of the sheep was risen from the dead and would go before them into Galilee, scene of His earthly life and of so much of His ministry. On their joyful way, the Risen Master Himself met the women. He salutes them: "Hail!". They bow in wonder and in worship, and hold Him reverently and adoringly by the feet. He tells them, as the angel did, "Be not afraid". He affectionately calls His disciples "my brethren", and repeats the angel's message that He will meet them in Galilee.

Meanwhile, some of the frightened guards had recovered sufficiently to go into the city to advise the chief priests as to what has happened. They seemed to know that what had happened was of greater importance for the chief priests than for Pilate. This was bad news indeed for the Sanhedrin. The priests bribed the soldiers. It was to the advantage of priests and soldiers alike that the people should not know the real truth, so a story was invented and the soldiers were bribed to tell the lie. They were to say that while they slept the disciples had come and had stolen the body. What a foolish story it was! Were they admitting to sleeping while on guard? Had they all slept? Professional, trained soldiers! They could be court-martialled for such dereliction of duty. Then, if indeed they were asleep, how did they know that the disciples, or anyone else, had come? And if there was real evidence that the body had been stolen by the disciples, then why not arrest these men forthwith and recover the body? Surely, if it had been stolen, it must be secreted somewhere. The frightened soldiers took the money. It was a large sum, and they told the lie with the assurance that if the governor heard of it the priests would persuade him for their protection. They need not be anxious. Sadly, as Matthew says, the unlikely, incredible story was told and retold, and to this day it is believed by many Jews, and Gentiles, who seem to be willingly ignorant of the absurdity of it all. Nevertheless, it is ironical that the enemies of Jesus should bring a report which testified that the tomb was empty. Men may debate and argue, and offer their various theories and supposed explanations, but the fact that the tomb was empty has never ever been in question. It is, as has been said, "A stubborn fact!". Yet still to this present day, the great archenemy himself would influence men to doubt or deny the truth of the resurrection of the crucified One. Christ risen is the very heart of the Gospel message and it is in the interest of the devil that men should not believe it.

Eleven disciples then left for Galilee. There is a certain sadness in this expression, "the eleven". There had been twelve, but there had been a traitor among the twelve, a defector. Judas was the only one of the twelve who was not a Galilean. He was Judas Iscariot, Judas Ish-Kerioth, Judas the man of Kerioth, a village of Judea. The eleven knew Galilee well. It was their home country, as it was His, their Master's. They now return to Galilee, in obedience to His word and that of the angel.

The Lord meets them at the appointed place, on one of the hills of Galilee. So much of our Lord's ministry in this Gospel has been associated with mountains. The Mount of Beatitudes, the Mount of Olives, the Mount of Transfiguration, and others too. "How beautiful upon the mountains are the feet of him that bringeth good tidings, that publisheth peace" (Is 52.7). Now, at the close of His ministry, the Saviour will again meet His disciples on a mountain. When they saw Him, they did homage to Him, but still some hearts doubted. How weak is our faith, even in those precious moments when in grace He shows Himself to us.

Matthew does not tell the story of the ascension. He knew it well of course, but others will tell it. Matthew's Gospel is a portrait of the King, the story of the King and the Kingdom. It is fitting, then, that he should leave us with this lovely picture of the King on earth, among His people. In regal majesty the King proclaims His authority, "All power is given unto me in heaven and in earth". In what apparent weakness they had so recently seen Him die, rejected by Israel and crucified by Romans. Calvary was the crime of the Gentile and the guilt of the Jew. Together they had rejected the King, just as the second Psalm had predicted. How different now! Risen from the dead, all power committed to Him, the King will commission His servants for the proclamation of the Kingdom. They were but a remnant, these men, but they would go forth with a mandate from the King Himself. How much encouragement will these words bring to a remnant of a later day, as they too fulfil the great commission, preaching the Gospel of the Kingdom.

Nevertheless, we of this present interim period go forth similarly. The King's commission goes beyond the lost sheep of the house of Israel. His servants must go to all nations. They are to make disciples, baptising them in the Name of the Father, and of the Son, and of the Holy Spirit. All the authority of the great Tri-unity would be with them in their ministry. They must teach those who responded to their message to observe all that He had commanded them, and they had the assurance of His constant presence with them. The Gospel closes with that lovely promise, "Lo, I am with you always, even unto the end of the age".

What a story Matthew has given us. In his opening verse

he promised us, "The book of the generation of Jesus Christ, the son of David, the son of Abraham". He has faithfully fulfilled his promise and accomplished his intention. By inspiration, Matthew has rehearsed the story of Jesus the Messiah, destined for a throne of glory as the Son of David, but going by way of the altar of sacrifice as the Son of Abraham. Matthew has devoted his earliest chapters to the King's ancestry and advent. He has told us of the King's ambassador and of His anointing. He has recorded the details of the King's administration and His attributes. He has described the King's agony and His subsequent authority. He has brought us from those lowly beginnings of the Saviour's birth at Bethlehem, through the trial in the wilderness and a ministry of teaching, preaching, healing, and praying, to the final hours of suffering and death, and on to resurrection ground. As we come to the end of Matthew's lovely story, well might we sing –

> *Crown Him with many crowns,*
>   *The Lamb upon His throne;*
> *Hark how the heavenly anthem drowns*
>   *All music but its own;*
> *Awake, my soul, and sing*
>   *Of Him who died for thee,*
> *And hail Him as thy matchless King*
>   *Through all eternity.*

> *Crown Him the Lord of love;*
>   *Behold His hands and side;*
> *Rich wounds yet visible above*
>   *In beauty glorified;*
> *All hail, Redeemer, hail!*
>   *For Thou hast died for me:*
> *Thy praise shall never, never fail*
>   *Throughout eternity.*

Crown Him the Lord of life
   Who triumphed o'er the grave,
And rose victorious in the strife
   For those He came to save:
His glories now we sing,
   Who died and rose on high,
Who died eternal life to bring,
   And lives that death may die.

Crown Him the Lord of heaven,
   Enthroned in worlds above,
The King of kings to whom is given
   The wondrous name of Love:
His reign shall know no end,
   And round His pierced feet
Fair flowers of Paradise extend
   Their fragrance ever sweet.

Conclusion and Summary

So our meditations in Matthew's Gospel are concluded. It is indeed a right royal Gospel. Matthew has given us a majestic, regal treatise concerning the King and the Kingdom. Mark, Luke, and John have likewise recorded their own inspired accounts of Jesus, each in his own unique and special way, but this former tax collector for the Romans is also unique, portraying for us something of the life and the ministry, the death and the resurrection, of One who was the King of Israel.

That life had indeed a lowly beginning at Bethlehem. Those sad words, "no room", were uttered very early and Jesus was born in an outside place. Matthew nevertheless has proven the undisputed rights of the infant to the throne of His father David. He has carefully and diligently traced the ancestry of Jesus and has given his readers a detailed genealogy of the babe born of the maid from Nazareth. The lineage was clear for all to see, if they had a willingness to see.

Again and again in his Gospel Matthew has shown also that all that Jesus was, with all that He said, and all that He did, was in fulfilment of Old Testament predictions and prophecies. He had come! The Messiah and King long-promised for Israel had made His advent, but, sadly, Israel had not recognised Him. Their Scriptures abounded with references to Messiah and His ministry, but, alas, they still failed to appreciate Him when He came.

Early in that ministry Jesus had presented His manifesto. That "Sermon on the Mount" is recorded by Matthew with more detail than in any of the other Gospels. It is a magnificent outline of the character of those who inherit the Kingdom, and is essentially an exposition of the character of the King Himself.

Such a record of the manifestation of the King's power then follows. Miracle after miracle seemed surely to demonstrate that the King was among them in power. They saw Him cleanse the leper, give sight to the blind, and hearing to the deaf. They saw the lame walking at His word, they saw demons expelled and the dead raised, and still did not seem to know that He was the promised King, for whom they had waited.

The King did have a faithful few, a little remnant of the nation. They loved Him and followed Him, both men and women, mostly from Galilee. He had chosen them that they might be with Him and they seemed to be ever at His side. What companionship there had been during those days, what fellowship. They walked by the lakeside and sat on the hillside, they talked in the streets and in the fields. He explained and expounded the ways of God to them and on one occasion they had to exclaim, "What manner of Man is this!".

But eventually the end came. The evil intent of the leaders of the nation was at last realised and, after a long night of mockery and blasphemy, of malignant false accusations and much pain, the King was crowned with thorns and sentenced to death, and they crucified Him. Kinder hands took His body from the tree and laid Him in a garden tomb. The sepulchre was sealed and guarded, but all in vain, for on the third day the stone was rolled away, the tomb was empty save for the vacated grave-clothes, and the King was alive, risen from the dead.

How it must have thrilled Matthew to record those words of the risen Christ: "All power is given unto me"! In what apparent weakness He had been nailed to the cross. To many it spelled the end of Jesus of Nazareth, but, in fulfilment of His own Scriptures and His own words to His disciples, He rose from the dead. One day Israel and the nations will acknowledge His Messiahship. He must reign, and He will!